GOD
AND
MAMMON

Also by Lance Morrow

The Chief: A Memoir of Fathers and Sons
Heart: A Memoir
Fishing in the Tiber: Essays
America: A Rediscovery
Safari: Experiencing the Wild (with Neil Leifer)
Evil: An Investigation
*The Best Year of Their Lives: Kennedy, Johnson, and Nixon
    in 1948; Learning the Secrets of Power*
Second Drafts of History: And Other Essays

GOD
AND
MAMMON

CHRONICLES OF AMERICAN MONEY

LANCE MORROW

Encounter
BOOKS
New York • London

First American edition published in 2020 by Encounter Books,
an activity of Encounter for Culture and Education, Inc.,
a nonprofit, tax exempt corporation.
Encounter Books website address: www.encounterbooks.com

Manufactured in the United States and printed on
acid-free paper. The paper used in this publication meets
the minimum requirements of ANSI/NISO Z39.48–1992
(R 1997) (*Permanence of Paper*).

FIRST AMERICAN EDITION

LIBRARY OF CONGRESS CATALOGING-IN-PUBLICATION DATA

Names: Morrow, Lance, author.
Title: God and Mammon : Chronicles of American Money / by Lance Morrow.
Description: First American edition | New York : Encounter Books, 2020.
Identifiers: LCCN 2020021827 (print) | LCCN 2020021828 (ebook)
ISBN 9781641770965 (cloth) | ISBN 9781641770972 (epub)
Subjects: LCSH: Wealth—Social aspects—United States
Money—United States—Religious aspects.
Classification: LCC HC110.W4 M67 2020 (print) | LCC HC110.W4 (ebook)
DDC 306.30973—dc23
LC record available at https://lccn.loc.gov/2020021827
LC ebook record available at https://lccn.loc.gov/2020021828

Interior page design and typesetting by Bruce Leckie

In memory of my parents
Hugh Morrow and Elise Vickers McCormick

There swims in the American mind,
in depths where sunlight barely penetrates,
a fish seldom seen in the twenty-first century.
This is the sense of sin. It is a prehistoric creature; like the coelacanth,
all but extinct—a flickering remnant of the Calvinist.

Once, long ago, the scales of the fish were golden.
Now they are dull and obscure, like sunken Spanish bullion,
mossed over by centuries in the deep green sea.

The coelacanth of sin is not alone: it swims in the mind with a twin, a
shadow; and that consort is a sweeter, sadder thing—a sort of longing.

I

Thales of Miletus, the pre-Socratic Greek philosopher, astronomer, and mathematician, conceived that the earth is a flat disk floating on an infinite sea, and that the beginning of all things was water.

His student Anaximenes disagreed. He said the beginning of all things was air.

How did America begin? What was its primordial element?

I think it was money.

It was the desire for money. Money, broadly speaking, has been the logic of America: its mystique and raison d'être. It was the hope of money—the fantasy of it, the greed for it—that drew Europeans across the water. It was the ambition for money that sustained America and made it the richest and most powerful among the nations of the earth—although not the happiest. It was in the pursuit of money that Europeans—and other immigrants who followed on—subdued and overwhelmed the earlier continent and superimposed the America that we see now.

And it was because of money—exorbitant taxation—that the American colonists rebelled and demanded independence.

Money is an indelicate explanation of America, perhaps, but the truest one—or, anyway, the most intelligent starting point.

Other forces were at work as well—religious motives touched here and there by fanaticism; Bible stories still resonant, not yet obscure; remnants of Greece and Rome; the Enlightenment; ethnic traditions, darker tribal urges; geography, vast spaces opening westward; climate, which was on the whole seasonal, familiar, and nicely middling; firearms; technology; alcohol; the genius for tinkering.

But money, for better or worse, was the American protagonist, center stage—hero or villain. By and by, you had the Malefactors of Great Wealth and Horatio Alger's beamish boys. Race and religion—though each of them was very powerful, with deeper resonances than anything so crass and disreputable as money—were supporting actors. Wealth was the American star.

Money was not, technically, everything. But it was a great deal.

For the sake of simplicity—and for the sake of entertainment, too, since money is an entertaining subject—I'd like to suspend complexity and reduce everything, for a moment, to this one fundamental: money as the American thing.

Alexis de Tocqueville is my witness: "One usually finds that love of money is either the chief or a secondary motive at the bottom of everything the Americans do.... It agitates their minds but disciplines their lives."

Money became freedom's business partner, the demiurge of the entrepreneurial middle class that founded the country. Money was the American Shinto.

The New World was, in the words of another Frenchman, Hector Saint John de Crèvecoeur, "une feuille blanche," or a blank page—a fresh beginning of history, a story liberated from the old world's plotlines, the worn grooves of centuries. The Puritans came on "an errand into the wilderness"—a religious mission—but soon they set about clearing that wilderness, chopping down trees and selling the timber, and planting wheat, and digging for coal and iron and copper and silver and gold, and putting in railroads and great cities. Money took over as the organizing principle—not religion or birth, class or custom. Money found its apotheosis.

The country was abundant, hospitable, dangerous, and usually heartless—just as money is inclined to be: ruthless until it develops a conscience and goes in for Improvement. Crèvecoeur's New Man had unprecedented mobility. The newcomer might shed the old self and disappear into America and grow a new self. The New World was far enough away to sever the ties with Europe's still feudalistic restrictions. Money became the idiom of freedom and its partner, rapacity. It's here that we encounter the paradox of the freedom to enslave. The signature American melodrama of race originated in money—in the economics of sugar, molasses, rice, tobacco, indigo, cotton, and kidnapped black African labor.

That labor—referring to the African slaves—became an object, became property and commodity, and even became a medium of exchange. An entry in *Encyclopædia Britannica* would report: "Scores, perhaps hundreds of different objects have served as money at one time or another, including such things as slaves, gunpowder and the jawbones of pigs." *Objects*! Such *things*! The three mediums of exchange seemed to summarize an underthread of American history: slaves, gunpowder, the jawbones of pigs.

🐖

The booster spoke of "the fruited plain." The bitter realist said, "Root, hog, or die." The elegiac intellectual turned away from the spectacle in disgust.

You can't go wrong, in any case, if you think about America in terms of binaries, twins—contradictions that collaborate in the national scheme of things, like positive and negative charges of electricity. America was always to have an aspect of Dr. Jekyll and Mr. Hyde, of God and Mammon, of innocence and sin.

This study approaches the partnership of God and Mammon in both its historical and contemporary dimensions—on the vertical and the horizontal axes, as it were. The vertical axis is American history. The horizontal axis follows events in the extraordinary year 2020. The two dimensions take turns in the narrative.

The triumphs of American money have been great. I talk also about its failures and limitations—and about values that lie beyond money's capacity to measure, meanings that cannot be grasped in money's language.

And the book is about a theological error—an evil, slavery—introduced an eon ago, when America was a garden, and about how to evaluate that long-ago sin and its effect upon the country now.

In 2020, in the midst of a pandemic, America would accuse itself bitterly on the subject of race—would beat its breast in paroxysms of self-hatred, of ostentatious remorse.

We encounter more binaries.

What if the narrative of a sinful and uniquely racist 21st-century America was wrong? Is it not a fallacy and a wild exaggeration—Fake News—to proceed on the premise that the lives of black Americans of the 21st century are indistinguishable in their afflictions from the lives of their great-great-great-great-great-grandparents? Has not America, over many years, succeeded in helping African Americans to achieve what are—by any standard in any country in the world—remarkable levels of prosperity, education, citizenship, and political power? What if the paroxysms of 2020 represent not truth telling but error? What if they amount merely to a wanton assault upon the country at a moment when it is suffering and vulnerable?

In 1702, Cotton Mather preached that the Christian must row to heaven with two oars—the oar of his spiritual calling and the oar of his material calling. If he pulls on only one of them, the boat goes in circles and the Christian can never reach the safe harbor of salvation.

The idea of the two oars, accommodating Puritan theology to commercial practice, would eventually become the national doctrine. It was not enough for Americans to do well; in theory, they must also do good, and *be* good. By "be good," I do not mean merely that they must behave themselves; I mean that they must strive to be virtuous in the demanding sight of God. They must justify America's great fortune—and find some deeper purpose for it.

❧

American Virtue would ask: "But what of race? Can a people be good if they enslave fellow creatures who are fashioned in the image of God and share in the divinity bestowed on the slave owner—or three-fifths of it, anyway? Could the slave owners ever have been virtuous? Did God look the other way while this was going on? Did his justice sleep? If America was so good, how could it be so evil?"

Mammon would look up in irritation and reply: "That was all a long time ago. Things happened between then and now—a Civil War, for example, and the thorough and transforming civil rights acts of the 1960s. Anyway, to be less parochial in our perspective, slavery has been around, in most parts of the world, forever—since the beginning of human cruelty and greed and power. Beware of sanctimony. If you wish to speak about Africa, catching people and holding them in brutal servitude was the way of the chiefs long before the white man came. Beware of naïve perfectionism. Beware of anachronism, of self-righteousness. Beware of getting drunk on indignation. There's a good fellow."

🍂

Cotton Mather published his *Magnalia Christi Americana* [Christ's Great Deeds in America]: *The Ecclesiastical History of New-England from Its First Planting in the Year 1620, until the Year of Our Lord 1698*. He traced the rapid evolution of New England from the austere and punitive piety of the first settlement to middle-class prosperity and the beginnings of American abundance, with a glimpse, farther off on the horizon, of the fortunes that would emerge, for example, from whaling and the China trade.

Mather fretted that money had already gotten the upper hand. He wrote: "Religion brought forth prosperity, and the daughter destroyed the mother. . . . [T]here is danger lest the enchantments of this world make [the colonists] forget their errand into the wilderness."

But Mather committed the matricide that he condemned. He rhapsodized about the American profusion—as evidence of God's grace and ingenuity—and yet captured and assigned a price, for example, to the innumerable passenger pigeons that profligate Americans would, in time, cause to become extinct:

> I will add a Curiosity relating to the Pidgeons, which annually visit
> my own Country in their seasons, in such incredible numbers, that
> they have commonly been sold for Two-pence a dozen; yea, one Man
> has at one time surprized no less than two hundred dozen in his

Barn, into which they have come for Food, and by shutting the door,
he has had them all.

And so it came to pass. The daughter slew the mother. The enchantment of money overpowered religious zeal, gentrified it, and confined it
to the Sabbath—ceding to piety one-seventh of the week and giving over
the other days to Mammon.

The riches of America in this world would outshine the promised glory
of the next. The busy, gaudy, dangerous actuality of America, once it got its
economy organized, would prove more absorbing than the promise of eternity. Here was the secularized fulfillment of God's promise, the rainbow and
the pot of gold at the end of it. Boastful, prideful America would learn to
think of itself as the next best thing to heaven—eschatology without doom.

Money—being so flexible and adaptable to all particular needs and
stories—was the star of the promise and the vehicle of its fulfillment. In
1925, President Calvin Coolidge, whose ancestors included passengers
on the Mayflower and defendants in the Salem witch trials, told the
National Association of Newspaper Editors: "After all, the chief business
of the American people is business. They are profoundly concerned with
producing, buying, selling, investing and prospering in the world."

So it was that money—working soft, seductive erosions, caressing the
original theology—would resolve the estrangement between Calvinism
and the Enlightenment. The American prosperity would, in time, bring
forth Thomas Jefferson's spacious trinity "Life, liberty and the pursuit of
happiness." Jonathan Edward's "angry God" ascended into the upper air
of Deism—in the same way, as it were, that in India's hot months the
British Raj withdrew to cool itself in the foothills of the Himalayas, at
Simla.

Happiness could be simplified to mean money and what it could
buy. It was assumed that life and liberty would, in the natural course
of things, lead on to happiness. Money—although a temperamental
thing, subject to violent mood swings—was the energy on which
the American Dream would proceed down the years. Money and
the Constitution were the two indispensable tools in the advance of
American civilization.

By the time the Christian urgencies waned and America became more diverse and secular, the pretension to virtue had embedded itself as an item of national pride and patriotic vanity, even as the process of money-getting continued in its eager, acquisitive, and Mammonish ways. This went on until, in the Gilded Age after the Civil War, money performed a garish mutation and became colossal. America commenced being a superpower.

Whatever its worldly guise, the essence of the American idea remained very much as it was in Cotton Mather's image of two oars: to reconcile God and Mammon—even to set them up as partners in the rowing toward heaven. Alter the metaphor: Church and state may have been legally separated by the First Amendment, but virtue and money have had a long, quarrelsome, indissoluble marriage, so to speak—one marked by hypocrisy, chronic infidelity, and, at the same time, some remarkably admirable results.

Money—I mean, inequality as to who has money and who does not—became one of the country's two permanent moral dilemmas. The other is race. The two conundrums were bound up with each other. Some of the great fortunes emerged from the slave trade. Newport, Rhode Island, with its magnificent "cottages" of the rich of the Gilded Age, was in an earlier time founded, to a significant degree, by money earned in the African slave trade. Balzac wrote in *Père Goriot*: "Le secret des grandes fortunes sans cause apparente est un crime oublié, parce qu'il a été proprement fait." The thought would be rendered more simply thus: "Behind every great fortune, there is a great crime."

The descendants of slaves were among the poorest, the ones without money. There was always trouble when Americans tried to reconcile their materialism with their theology. I will write about the Brown brothers, Moses and John, of the wealthy Rhode Island merchant family who gave its name to Brown University. Moses was an abolitionist. John was active in the African slave trade. Somehow the two brothers managed to remain brotherly and proceed with their enterprises, even as they conducted one of the earliest and bitterest of arguments about whether American virtue could be squared with the buying and selling of human beings.

Race in America began as a drama of money, originating in the economics of cotton, tobacco, sugar, rum, and the Middle Passage.

A key American story, *Huckleberry Finn*, contains this sardonic riff: The runaway Jim has a happy moment when he reasons that, as a slave, he would fetch $800 on the market, and, in consequence, being now fled from bondage and at liberty, he will be a rich man! He rejoices to find that he is worth $800.

American history here and there indulges in a sly play of coincidences. We find two antithetical John Browns in the American scheme, for example—the slave merchant of Providence and his antiself, the wild abolitionist martyr of Harper's Ferry. In 1954, Earl Warren's Supreme Court would end—or try to end—the racial segregation of American public schools in its ruling in *Brown v. Board of Education*. And there was the Brown Brothers' slave ship called *Sally*, which made a disastrous voyage to the Windward Coast of Africa in 1764 (more than half the slaves perished in the Middle Passage, some of them killed in an abortive rebellion on the high seas) that would precipitate the tremendous moral debate between the slaver John Brown and the abolitionist Moses Brown—God and Mammon wrestling each other for years in the New England conscience. The slave ship *Sally* would become a sort of premonition of Sally Hemings, the half-sister of Thomas Jefferson's dead wife, Martha—Sally was one of Jefferson's slaves and, years after Martha's demise in 1782, also his mistress and the mother of his children, who were to be both his offspring and his property. Jefferson and Hemings became another of the founding stories—though it would be long concealed or half-concealed.

Nature organizes itself in binaries—male and female, to start. Could it be that Thomas Jefferson and Sally Hemings were the American Adam and Eve?

Nature flourishes and advances itself in dynamics of contradiction. That is one reason that the energy produced by the discrepancy in the American mind between the call of God and the work of Mammon has, time after time, been the engine of American civilization.

American money is a large subject. Lytton Strachey explained the method he employed in writing *Eminent Victorians*, his collection of biographical sketches of figures in 19th-century England. Strachey advised: "If he is wise . . . [the explorer of the past] will row out over [the] great ocean of material, and lower down into it, here and there, a little bucket, which will bring up to the light of day some characteristic specimen, from those far depths, to be examined with a careful curiosity."

In this book, I lower my bucket and bring up a few characteristic specimens to examine—a shark, the odd hermit crab, a dolphin or octopus or lobster: a modest catch of people and ideas.

When I mentioned Strachey's metaphor of sea creatures just now, I remembered the scene in Theodore Dreiser's novel *The Financier* in which the ruthless money man, Frank Cowperwood, whom Dreiser based on the financier and convicted white-collar criminal Charles Yerkes, witnesses the struggle between a squid and a lobster in a Philadelphia market's fish tank, the lobster slowly devouring the squid, piece by piece. Cowperwood takes it to be a parable of the elemental struggle of money: "The squid couldn't kill the lobster—he had no weapon. The lobster could kill the squid—he was heavily armed. There was nothing for the squid to feed on; the lobster had the squid as prey. What was the result to be?"

For some reason, people identify money with fish and animals. Dollars have been called "clams" or "fish"—liquid assets, you see—and, of course, there are always the "bulls" and "bears." In talking of the vocabulary of money, I might also mention the numerous religious puns embedded in it—*save, redeem, period of grace*, and *goods*—meaning merchandise, not virtues. Religion and emotions: During the Great Depression, F. Scott Fitzgerald would speak of his "emotional bankruptcy" (another double meaning, connecting the economic with the psychological).

In this essay about money—a causerie, not the presentation of a formal thesis, because I do not think that money behaves in a coherent or formal way; and, even if it did, I would not be qualified to write about it (the worst grade I got in college was in a required economics-for-idiots course that was incomprehensible to me from the first class to the final exam)—I'm guided by something that Tocqueville wrote in a letter to a friend: "It is less the facts that I am looking for...than the traces of the movement of ideas and sentiments."

An essay is an attempt to think a subject through. All soliloquys in Shakespeare are succinct and tightly reasoned essays, for example, in which the private mind, conversing with itself—struggling with itself—goes to work to analyze a public and universal subject. Think of Hamlet's "To be or not to be," for example, which, in 260 words, manages to consider the same subject upon which, say, Jean-Paul Sartre's *Being and Nothingness* would lavish ten or fifteen million (who bothered to count Sartre's words?). The notion is to grope from personal dilemma toward universal truth—to connect private experience to the larger public drama. Michel de Montaigne, inventor of the modern essay, labored brilliantly and interminably and sometimes incoherently to connect his private experience (his cat, his kidney stones, his readings in the classics, his bowel movements) with universal truths.

The idea is to capture money in vivo, to suggest the part that this boisterous, decisive, gaudy, mysterious, frequently treacherous, neurotic, and vanishing thing has played in forming the American character. I am especially interested in American money in its connection to race, and to the evil time when flesh was money.

It's the emotions of money that interest me. Think of the emotions of race as they reverberate through the private and public layers of the nation's life. Think about ideas that emerge as money intersects with the American mind.

Mr. Micawber revealed his life's lesson to David Copperfield, who was Dickens's young alter ego: "Annual income twenty pounds, annual expenditure nineteen [pounds] nineteen [shillings] and six [pence], result happiness. Annual income twenty pounds, annual expenditure twenty pounds ought and six, result misery."

Micawber laid out money's binaries of happiness and misery. Those are the two extremes. Money also offers complicated variations—the ecstasy of windfall; the despair of ruin; the apathy, boredom, or dullness that may attend poverty or, counterintuitively, may plague wealth. The anxiety of want. The plump nuances of complacency.

I write this in the early days of the coronavirus pandemic. The mood is dark enough—the economy stunned; the world changed, turned upside down.

Dickens, bard of sentiment and sentimentality, gave to the subject of money his most intense emotions—of longing, anxiety, fear, fulfillment: his memories of the Marshalsea prison and the blacking factory. Dickens had a genius for bringing money, as well as weather and cities and inanimate objects, especially houses, alive with glowing or piercing vivacity. There was such a thing as Dickensian Shinto (to use that shimmering word again)—so that even an entire city, fogbound London, might be suffused with uncanny moral animation. *A Christmas Carol* (teeming with ghosts, regrets, time travel, sin, the miracle of renewal) amounts to a brilliant sermon and legal argument in favor of emotions—love, the Christmas spirit—as the key to salvation and the annulment and washing away of sin. Only emotion—the wassail, the dancing, the Christmas goose, goodwill—will gain dominion over cold, hard money and the soul-destroying vice of greed. Only emotion will cause Tiny Tim to walk again—the miracle that is the climax of a story about Christ's birthday.

J. P. Morgan purchased the original manuscript of *A Christmas Carol* and kept it in the library of his mansion on 36th Street in Manhattan—a trophy of sentiment in his magnificent plunder. Morgan worked the ruthless and emotionless Mammon side of human operations. The sacred and profane aspects of American money have always been in wary negotiation with each other, much like the Brown brothers of Providence debating the pros and cons of the slave trade. Paradoxically, great sins have sometimes brought forth miracles of virtue, and crimes have made new innocence possible. Redemption is the word. Money may be redeemed in the religious as well as the financial sense. Money, for all its tendency toward corruption, has also been the patron of excellence, magnificence. Did John D. Rockefeller go to heaven? Andrew Carnegie gave all of those libraries to the country. Did that save his soul?

The emotions with which money is charged, as if with electricity, become flesh in money's transactions. They coalesce in stories. The American desire for money created an American culture of money—an obsession that became the national way of life. It's true that at times American money behaves like a mere dull clerk in an eyeshade, but, just as often, it breaks loose and plays the genius, often a ruthless one, and sometimes a crazy one. Money's range has been Shakespearean, Homeric.

The charm and the danger of emotions is their disorder. Money, you might say, amounts to a complex interface of the private self with the public world. It pretends to proceed intelligently, even scientifically. But it's a rough beast when it's off the leash.

Money is a rational, routine instrument of society, a public convenience; but it also has an alien life of its own. Sometimes it behaves not unlike a pandemic. It may proceed by its own logic—which may be the disorderly logic of dreams.

Money does business constantly in the realm of superstition, where it may flourish or perish. What's the stock market about, if not clairvoyance? Here is a story of eerie premonition:

In late summer of 1928, on August 28—two years before he received the Nobel Prize for literature—Sinclair Lewis, author of the iconic American money fable *Babbitt*, returned from Europe; visited the offices of his publisher, Harcourt, Brace; and, looking down onto Madison Avenue, made this prediction: "Within a year, this country will have a terrible financial panic. . . . I don't think, I know. Can't you see it? Can't you smell it? I can see people jumping out of windows on this very street."

2

The coronavirus arrived like a dream—surreal, incredible—with vast consequences. It became an immense fact of economics as well as public health. It came upon the world repeating, as it spread, the warning of the prophet Amos: "Woe to them that are at ease in Zion." It savored of the Book of Revelation. The virus was the Beast. (Here we are again among the animal metaphors.)

I recalled a beast from a different text. Near the beginning of a Sherlock Holmes story called "The Adventure of the Sussex Vampire," Holmes remarks, "Matilda Briggs was not the name of a young woman, Watson. It was a ship which is associated with the giant rat of Sumatra, a story for which the world is not yet prepared." The vampire story continues, and no one (neither Holmes, nor Watson, nor Arthur Conan Doyle) mentions the giant rat of Sumatra again. The effect is eerie. The rat lingers in the reader's mind: a dire possibility, latent in the world.

And so, the coronavirus turned up a century later. The giant rat of Sumatra came 'round at last.

Never has America been so filled with parables of money—warning riddles, money adaptations of the dilemma of theodicy, variations on the theme of money's wild impermanence: Now you see it, now you don't. The pandemic has declared that anything is possible and it implies, to those of religious instinct, that God has either withdrawn from the world or else has been moved—by what exactly?—to chastise the sins of mankind in a particularly thorough way.

The pandemic, followed by the Black Lives Matter disturbances that swept the country after the death of George Floyd at the hands of police in Minneapolis, has carried the country into a new dimension, a new era.

Michael Bloomberg, the former mayor of New York City, spent more than half-a-billion dollars in the brief hallucination that was his hundred-day presidential primary campaign in 2020. The result was crickets—very expensive crickets. (*More animals!*) He came away with nothing more to show for such extravagance than a few pledged delegates from American Samoa. The immense gesture—$600 million spent in a wink, which some said would be as much as $1 billion when you added up the bills—had the surreal quality of a gambler's all-or-nothing plunge at the tables in Monte Carlo. In such a drama, one might have expected that as dawn came up, the sound of a pistol shot would be heard offstage. But Mike Bloomberg was not the suicidal type; and anyway, he had a lot more money where that came from. He was said to have a net worth of $60 billion, even after his campaign fiasco.

What was the lesson of such a humbling, if that is what it was? Partly, I suppose, it taught that money cannot buy the presidency—not Bloomberg's money anyway. How does one read it when, presently, the financial damage caused by the pandemic—trillions down the drain and trillions dispensed to try to stop it—seems to confirm the Bloomberg inference that all money calculations, and money itself, may be a game of illusions; a mockery of the very idea of measurable value?

❧

It is March 12, 2020, just after dawn on my farm, which lies between two ridges on a dirt road in a valley in upstate New York.

From my window, in gray, gathering light, I see a red fox crossing the field on the other side of the stone wall. He moves with the bouncy and characteristic lope of a fox in late winter, early spring—the last of the mating season. At this time of year, the fox is gregarious, full of curiosity. His eye catches my movement behind the window glass and he pauses and stares at the farmhouse in an amiable way, as if waiting to see if I will come out and play. After a long moment, he lopes on down the game trail toward the creek.

I turn back to the screens.

Yesterday, the World Health Organization declared the coronavirus to be a pandemic.

It begins.

Wall Street is not yet open for the day's business, but in the world's other time zones, markets are crashing. The American university system has begun abruptly shutting down (Harvard, MIT, Columbia, Ohio, Michigan, nearly everyone else). Classes will be held online. The NCAA has canceled its March Madness basketball tournaments. Shutting down basketball seems obscurely unthinkable and, in a funny way, is more troubling to the mind than the market's dive.

There are video clips from a television speech from the Oval Office last night.

President Trump reads from a teleprompter without tone or expression. His address to the nation has the atmosphere of a hostage video. Flights from continental Europe will be suspended for a month, he announces dully. He proclaims government interventions here and there.

The markets notice his countenance and body English, his "affect" or lack thereof. Traders attend shrewdly to his voice, measuring the implications. They find the president to be lifeless, reluctant, as if he disowns the moment, as if his mind has fled entirely elsewhere.

Trump seems to have understood just enough for his instincts to be privately alarmed to a public danger that he does not yet fathom or care to acknowledge, because he had so much riding on the alternative, on his triumphant scenario.

Donald Trump is the strangest and most ineffable of American presidents. Only a few weeks ago, he was impeached by the House of Representatives and acquitted by the Senate. Despite all that (or because of all that), he had a plausible hope of reelection in November. The likely Democratic nominee, seventy-seven-year-old Joe Biden, the former vice president, shaped up as a fragile, accident-prone, muddled remnant of an earlier time, an earlier America altogether. Despite recent primary victories, he was not embraced by his divided party but rather, for want of a better idea, accepted with a desperate acquiescence—the desperation emerging from a fear that his nearest competitor, Vermont senator

Bernie Sanders, an even older man, a red-diaper socialist whose utterances savored of the Popular Front, might get the nomination.

Trump until a moment ago was astride a bull economy—the Dow at 28,000, unemployment at record lows. Such an economy expressed crass, braying, hard-charging Trump himself—who was either a notorious liar and vulgarian or else a hero and populist truth teller, depending on which political side you embraced in the struggles of a divided country.

Donald Trump may amount to the very apotheosis of American money: of its brash metaphysics and effrontery. An incarnation and unflattering caricature of it, or a throwback to the Gilded Age—to characters (in one reading of him) like Daniel Drew or Jay Cooke or Jay Gould or Jim Fisk or Collis Huntington: beasts of the prime, masterpieces of sleek amorality. In the contrary interpretation, Trump is the fierce, rough-cut, and principled original who stood between the country's true self and the perverted innovations of the coercive if not totalitarian Left, with its cult-like identity politics and its neurotic obsession with gender. For a man called uncouth and inarticulate by his enraged enemies, Trump managed to communicate perfectly with his faithful. He held his great rallies around the country enthralled with speeches that were not really speeches but jazz improvisations, half- and quarter-sentences, riffs of anecdote, satire. They loved him; they tolerated any seeming incoherence as adding up to a force on the right side of things. Even if they did not find his person or his manners lovable, it did not matter: They said, *The Left doesn't understand. We don't have to like him. He's our murder weapon.*

Despite everything, including his enemies' deepening hatred, he had been effective in important areas—the economy, deregulation, the appointment of numerous judges congenial to his conservative base: He was building a judicial wall, even if the physical one, down on the Mexican border, proceeded more fitfully.

But, all at once, the narrative line of Trump's presidency, the money success in which he gloried until a moment ago, has been disrupted. The coronavirus overwhelmed Wuhan, where it started, and spread to Italy and Spain and elsewhere on the globalized planet, crisscrossed by 93,000 flights daily (the flight paths as densely interwoven as the string around a baseball), and Trump in the Oval is delivering an address to the nation in which he sounds like a sullen adolescent who has just wrecked his father's Cadillac.

The country goes to sleep in a mood of foreboding.

◈

Thursday morning now, and Dow futures point to a loss of 1,100 points at the opening bell. An e-mail arrives from my son in Sydney, where it is fourteen hours in the future. "It's crazy here," James reports, "and no one knows the right policy response, Sydney has a weird paranoid edge about it." At a Woolworth's in Bondi Junction, people are fighting like savages over toilet paper.

What does it mean?

It is the beginning of the war, like the first Battle of Bull Run. People say either it will be an apocalypse—or else it will be over by Christmas. Hope and fear take turns in the mind.

Everyone searches for a pattern—first in the Dow, later in the accumulating numbers of the sick and the dead and in the geography of the spreading calamity (Wuhan, China, Italy, Spain, and so on around the infected, blotching globe). I think of W. H. Auden's splendid, mordant poem "The Fall of Rome":

Unendowed with wealth or pity,
Little birds with scarlet legs,
Sitting on their speckled eggs,
Eye each flu-infected city.

Three days ago, the Dow lost 2,000 points—the steepest drop since the financial crisis of 2008. Next morning, the Dow talked itself into a rebound of 800 points, cheered a little by the president's promise to suspend payroll tax deductions and provide help for hourly workers who are knocked off the job by the coronavirus.

Now the Dow thinks more about it and the mood changes: inklings of panic. Algorithms tremble. Skittish players start selling, until the index subsides into negative numbers again.

From the White House, a crisis call goes out to the presidents of the country's biggest insurance companies. They flap in from everywhere on corporate jets, and just before noon the nation sees them on television with Trump—corporate dukes and earls, honchos who are at the same time ordinary Americans of prosperous middle age hunched around the enormous table in the Cabinet Room as if summoned to an emergency luncheon of the Rotary Club. The president makes soft, grim noises (voice hoarse, the Donald as Vito Corleone) meant to sound reassuring—*There will be no insurance deductibles for treatment of the virus*, for example. *De rent stay-sa like before! The widow can keep her dog!*

These things are happening in real time. The Dow, seeing such gestures, briefly hopeful again, struggles up out of the negative. Presently it is 300 points to the good—and climbing. Trump's black motorcade (the shining and flashing black mamba, or the funeral procession, of his power: Charlemagne on his elephant) sweeps up Pennsylvania Avenue, past the Trump Hotel—that touch of Babylon—to the Capitol, where the president takes lunch with leaders of Congress.

By the end of the day, the Dow Jones Industrial Average has calmed itself with smelling salts and intimations of the old normal—a sense that pretty soon, maybe, the economy will wake up from this bad dream and things will be all right again. It is up 1,300 points.

The Dow looks like the electrocardiogram bouncing and dancing on the wall of an ICU: It registers fears and hopes with hysterical sensitivity; it responds to each gust of news or rumor, each spurt of adrenaline or passing shadow. It spooks and bucks like a horse that has heard a rattle-snake. It quavers neurotically, like Blanche DuBois in the second act of *A Streetcar Named Desire.*

Yesterday, or a few days ago, before all this started, there was jeering exuberance. Today, there is animal panic.

The market is not the economy, people say. It is a canary in a tornado.

It's right that money and the markets should suggest still another animal metaphor: Animals—pure, unmediated life-forms—may also be allegories, moving through the jungle of the world carrying messages of which they are entirely unaware. They are living ideas. Money, too, is a living creature and living idea, and inherently allegorical.

The first chapter of *Walden*—a chapter entitled "Economy"—contains this enigmatic sentence: "I long ago lost a hound, a bay horse, and a turtle dove, and am still on their trail." No one knows what Thoreau meant by the hound, bay horse, and turtle dove. People have tried to guess. He did not mean money but something opposite to money, prior to money—something irrecoverable and haunting. He meant the past, I think—an American past that was haunting precisely because it was nonexistent, uncreated. He went on: "Many are the travellers I have spoken concerning them, describing their tracks and what calls they answered to. I have met one or two who had heard the hound, and the tramp of the horse, and even seen the dove disappear behind a cloud, and they seemed as anxious to recover them as if they had lost them themselves."

The market—a hectic creature of the present—is not the objective correlative of the economy. Call it the *subjective* correlative—madly intuitional. Animals are subjective life-forms—when did you ever meet a dog with an objective mind? And money is the most subjective of all living things. There are times when money even seems to be a sort of hysterical virus, born of dead bats and pangolins in wet markets on the other side of the world.

Think about an ultimate version of the subjective correlative of money—Midas, the Phrygian king whom Dionysus (in gratitude for a favor) granted a wish (an iconically and ironically foolish one): that whatever he touched would turn to gold. That answered prayer was regretted soon enough. The king turned each rose in his rose garden to gold at his touch, and this miracle made him giddy for an hour. Then, by and by, he found that his touch turned his food and wine to gold, so that he could not eat or drink. And when he touched his daughter, she, too, turned to gold.

Be careful: True alchemy turns greed into tragedy. That is the killjoy moral of the tale. Midas is ruthlessly corrected by reality, which wags its finger and says, *I told you so.* Money, even more than sex, invites moralism. Midas is the origin parable of the truth that *money cannot make you happy.*

And yet, America denies that maxim. That's the whole point of the country. America was founded on the idea that money can indeed make you happy—and that, in fact, it does! *It must!* It can make an entire country happy. All advertising—trillions of dollars' worth, the immense inundation of playlets and parables, the brilliant art form and true psychic surround of media—is based on the idea that money (that is, the products that money buys) will make you happy. That's the promise at the heart of American money.

Money can even make the country as a whole *virtuously* happy. Wealth rose up a mighty nation, the United States of America. It created mighty American families—lords of fortune who reversed the lesson of Midas. It is true that when the Phrygian turned his food and wine and his very daughter into gold, the outcome was tragic and ironic, a smiting lesson administered by fate and designed to tell you not to wish for too much in this life. Beware of answered prayers, it said. But the Rockefellers in the second generation turned John D.'s vast wealth—however sharply or piratically acquired—into universities, museums, parks, and other benefactions; and that was a great good. The Ludlow Massacre was redeemed, a generation later, by the Cloisters and by cancer cures advanced at the Rockefeller Institute.

Midas was a Phrygian. John D. Rockefeller was an American. That is the difference between them—the difference between the blight of the Midas touch and the benefactions of the Rockefeller touch.

You must be careful what you wish for. Midas was not careful. He was a fool. He was Daffy Duck at Aladdin's cave: "I'm rich! I'm rich! I'm thocially thecure!" (So much in the drama of money lends itself to cartoons.)

Yet, on the other hand, you may, like the Rockefellers, have gold in Midas-like abundance but, contrary to the ancient trope, still be wise and good and intelligent in your philanthropies. Bill and Melinda Gates proceed on such benevolent models, with such hope.

American money is of Mammon, Americans may tell themselves on Sundays; but the American faith holds that money may also please God and accomplish his work, while pleasing Americans themselves by giving them a good life. America, in short, went about rewriting Christ's teachings, revising the ones about how it is easier for a camel to pass through a needle's eye than for a rich man to enter the Kingdom of Heaven, and about how the first shall be last.

>

Now, in the time of pandemic, people fear to touch doorknobs or shake another's hand, lest the touch, by the new and immensely perverse alchemy—an evil version of the Midas touch—turn into virus and death.

Nature seems to have imposed some immense but unintelligible rebuke. What does it mean? Anything?

The poor are trapped in the cities. So are many of the rich. The butler who brings the martini may also be carrying the disease. The stealthy virus seeks out both groups equally—the rich and the poor—except, of course, that many people with money have withdrawn to their second homes in the country, thus also infecting the countryside. On the island of Vinalhaven in Penobscot Bay off the coast of Maine just yesterday, the local, year-round residents dropped a tree to block the driveway of some summer people who had fled the big city early in the season, in March, for the refuge of their island home. The tree in effect quarantined the rich city people inside their island vacation house, lest they infect the poorer locals.

>

The writer Alex Shoumatoff—whose mother was Elizabeth Shoumatoff, the artist who was in the act of painting Franklin Roosevelt's portrait in April of 1945 when he complained of a sudden, terrible headache and died in Warm Springs, Georgia—posts on Facebook this morning: "Money is killing the world, a Penan hunter-gatherer told me in Borneo in 2013."

Americans have always believed that money was good. But maybe Shoumatoff's hunter-gatherer in Borneo is right? Have climate change and the coronavirus formed an alliance to put the human race out of business?

Or anyway, what's the meaning of this enormous thing that is happening to the world? Death tolls mount, friends and family are taken, the world's economies shut down. Fortunes evaporate.

*

The pandemic is not more unsettling than the Lisbon earthquake of 1755. But even that relatively local apocalypse altered the Western mind. The quake occurred on All Saint's Day, November 1, in 1755. It killed perhaps fifty thousand. No one is certain of the death toll. The tsunami that followed the quake killed still more, and so did the conflagration that started when the heaving earth shook the churches and capsized the votive candles and set the town on fire.

In the aftermath, Voltaire wrote *Candide*, mocking Leibniz's idea of the "best of all possible worlds." The earthquake, which would have registered between 8 and 9 on the Richter Scale, reverberated in the world of ideas, in language and metaphor. Old solidities trembled. The very ground that people stood on—the ground of religious and philosophical belief—became treacherous, latent with danger, unbelief, apocalypse. There would be only thirty-four years between the Lisbon earthquake and the French Revolution.

We know that the coronavirus pandemic will alter the way that the world of the 21st century thinks and behaves. We don't know the details yet—they will evolve.

Forty-five years before Lisbon, the German philosopher Gottfried Wilhelm Leibniz invented the term *theodicy*, which means "vindication of God." Theodicy asked: *How can evil exist if God is all-good and all-powerful?* That was—and remains—the core dilemma of faith, the fierce Christian version of a Zen koan. After Lisbon, answers to that question became dazed or mordant and impious. Voltaire mocked Leibniz. The evils grew more elaborate over the centuries as technology got better at certain tasks—demonstrated by such events as the Somme and the Holocaust. The world improved (in science, medicine, knowledge, convenience, to name a few), but so did the efficiency of its wickedness.

Theologians used to draw a distinction between "natural evil" and "moral evil." Natural evil referred to earthquakes, floods, cancer, and other such "natural" afflictions for which human beings could not reasonably be blamed. Moral evil was the kind of evil that is, in one way or another, man's fault, not nature's or God's. Moral evil would be Auschwitz or Pol Pot's killing fields, to mention extreme examples.

If the coronavirus had been contained—if it had gone nowhere instead of proliferating worldwide, if it had remained an exotic laboratory hypothesis—then it would not even have made the evening news in America. Failure to contain the virus, however—failure to see the danger and to act in time—carried the matter over into the category of evils (torts of policy and management) for which humans may be held accountable.

Few people bother with theology or theodicy anymore. They speak of incompetence and stupidity and politics. We have abandoned the realm in which radical Evil (with a capital *E*) conjures up Lucifer and Satan, the tradition of profound metaphysical wickedness, something that remains attractive to the literary mind. We have descended instead into the contingencies of banal, lethal, and flawed reality—and flawed leaders.

Hannah Arendt addressed the descent some years ago. She coined the phrase "Banality of evil." In January of 1963—in the midst of controversy over her book *Eichmann in Jerusalem*—Arendt wrote a letter to Gershom Scholem, the great scholar of Jewish mysticism, in which she told him, "I . . . no longer speak of radical evil. . . . The fact is that today I think that evil in every instance is only extreme, never radical: It has no depth, and therefore has nothing demonic about it. Evil can lay waste to the entire world, like a fungus, growing rampant on the surface." That is where we are now—in the grips of an extreme but not theological fungus.

The epoch of the Anthropocene seems to have dispensed with the old distinction between natural evil and moral evil. Disruptions of nature—climate change, for example, or the coronavirus—are parsed as the consequence of human activity, of choices made by people, not by God or nature.

Still, there remains a residual temptation to see the coronavirus as inscrutable pushback—as a ferocious reality check. Is the pandemic some sort of cosmic rebuke? If so, a rebuke by whom—and of what? Or is the coronavirus morally meaningless? Is it merely a worldwide accident in which humankind has collided head on at eighty miles an hour with an 18-wheeler full of germs.

I just reread the profound and impossible story that begins, "There was a man in the land of Uz, whose name was Job."

Uz is us. The Book of Job remains inscrutable, though very beautiful in parts, especially in chapter 28, which begins, "Surely there is a vein for silver, and a place for gold where they fine it."

You might study the Book of Job for centuries without arriving at "the place of understanding." But you may love the book nonetheless, it seems to me—and be obscurely comforted by its ruthlessness, its devastation.

3

When I was a boy growing up in Washington, DC, I felt the emotions that money or the lack of it brings, the Dickens touch—a blighting weather that may fill, subvert, and torment a house. It was a cold wind that blew through the chinks in the walls in the bitterest winter. This was the residue of the Great Depression: a lingering fear and despair, the shock of that great collapse that formed the character of my parents and their generation. It might come in dreams—of a house disintegrating, walls collapsing, floors giving way underfoot; the laths and plaster and wiring exposed like the innards of London houses hit in the blitz, suddenly cross-sectioned and exposed. Or in dreams of one's teeth falling out, in slow motion, like gravestones going down. Sudden, humiliating vulnerabilities had infiltrated the mind, as a virus is absorbed in the body.

The term *post-traumatic stress disorder* would come into use only later on, but that is roughly what I am talking about. Memory of the trauma never quite left my parents or almost anyone else of their generation. It would return unexpectedly—an infection of spirit. It settled in the nerves, not so raw or violent as the reaction that would be set off later on in veterans of the wars in Vietnam and Iraq and Afghanistan when they heard a loud noise or the blades of a helicopter, but real nonetheless, a haunting. It would set off melodrama. It was a curse upon the House of America, and it lasted for a long time, even after World War II had put everyone to work and rescued the economy.

I have written about my parents before. They were part of my private myth system, but they were also mixed up with the public characters in the capital city, all actors in the narrative of senators and presidents and the story of a certain historical time that shimmers now in my mind like a mirage. They are long gone, and I think of them as part of a continuum of American stories. Saul Bellow wrote: "We all need our memories. They keep the wolf of insignificance from the door."

&

My parents were a handsome pair—gifted, heedless, extravagant, and precocious, though absurdly young. They drank too much because everyone else drank too much, and because they were young enough and strong enough to shrug off its effects and wake up the next morning bright as dimes. In their favorite movie, *Casablanca*—released in 1942, when the Axis was on the march and winning everywhere, and the world seemed lost—alcohol figured in nearly every scene, a kind of sacrament and a reassuring companion on the desperate journey toward Lisbon, toward America, which was a radiance on the horizon that promised to usher the refugees into something like the Kingdom of God—only better, because ... more real.

The film is a Big Rock Candy Mountain of booze: Champagne cocktails. Cointreau. Brandy. "Boorbin," as Humphrey Bogart pronounced the word (he came from a family on the Philadelphia Main Line). *Casablanca* amounted to a religious romance and a gloriously cornball disquisition upon love and ethics and how to behave if you happen to be occupied by Nazis: *Play the Marseillaise!*

Casablanca had the background resonance—the moral authority, as it were—of the Great Depression and its politics, including the Spanish Civil War, Rick Blaine having been involved on the Republican, anti-fascist side. The movie was filled with a theology of sacrifice, selflessness, the greater love. Alcohol was the stuff of courage, a secular *sanguinis Christi*. That night in his office, Rick got drunk not in order to forget—but rather to remember—Paris.

When my mother and father were married in 1937, he was twenty-one and she was fifteen. *Fifteen*. They were sophisticated children—avid and toughened by the reality and danger of bad times. He smoked Camels, and squinted through the blue-gray smoke, and talked sometimes like Bogart (the slightly simian gangster Bogart, Duke Mantee). They picked up some of their moral standards and role models in movies, or in books (my mother, who never went to college and felt shame because of that, was a voracious autodidact, chaotically well read), even while the great drama that they witnessed, and from which they learned, played itself out in front of them every day in the White House and the Capitol and the drama of the world war.

My father was a newspaperman who covered the White House for the *Philadelphia Inquirer*, in Franklin Roosevelt's third term. He and the other reporters would crowd around FDR's desk in the Oval Office and throw questions at him—softballs mostly, about battlefronts abroad and government at home. The president—whom my father revered as a great man and satirized as a con artist who talked like W. C. Fields if Fields had gone to Harvard—would put on a performance. He would wag his great head and flourish his cigarette in the ivory cigarette holder, so that the smoke curled in a helix about his head while he improvised, as it were, upon his clarinet and violin and slide trombone.

My father was fond of John O'Hara's novel *Appointment in Samarra* and would act out the scene in which the small-time hood Al Grecco looks down upon Gibbsville, Pennsylvania, at Christmastime and snarls, "Merry Christmas, you stuck-up bastards. Merry Christmas from Al Grecco!"

It was a scene filled with the 1930s emotion of money. It anticipated the moment in 1936 when, in a campaign address at Madison Square Garden, Roosevelt, shaking his fist at the "bourbons" (he pronounced it *BUHHHH-bins)* and the "economic royalists" (vocabulary that he borrowed from the French Revolution), cried: "I welcome their hatred!" That was FDR—the Hudson River squire, Sarah Roosevelt's polio-stricken boy, with his twelve-pound leg braces, pince-nez glasses, and defiant chin—playing Spartacus, the outlaw man of the people, as he snarled, "Merry Christmas, you stuck-up bastards!"

I was born in September of 1939, three weeks after Hitler marched into Poland. My earliest memories are of Washington, DC, during the Second World War. There was a housing shortage because of the war and because of all the new people who were flocking into town—soldiers, bureaucrats, people connected with the war industries. We lived in a tiny house way out across the Anacostia River, on Benning Road Southeast, by the Maryland line. The landlord was a man named Mr. Basada—a figure of vague fear, a sort of ogre. Even at the age of four, I was aware of when the rent was due, or overdue, and there wasn't enough money to pay it (my parents would argue about it). Mr. Basada would come around to collect. An ominous cloud of a man appeared on our tiny front porch. He wore a black overcoat and had a wart on his nose, and eyes like black grapes.

In later years, Benning Road, in Washington's Ward 8, would be part of Marion Berry's home territory and a battleground in the terrible drug wars. Young blacks died there by the scores, gunning one another down in disputes over turf. The funerals went on and on, and the boys' mothers and grandmothers, who still had the sweet, old-fashioned church connections they had brought up from the South, dressed in their Sunday clothes (a tragic, festive brightness) and wept over the boys' coffins in the A.M.E. churches.

During the Second World War, in the first few years of my life, there was rationing, and there were blackout curtains on our windows when people still feared that German bombers might make it across the Atlantic and, guided by the lights in our windows, hammer Washington as they had devastated London. Small flags with stars appeared in windows in houses up and down the block—a star for each man or boy of the house who had gone to war: a gold star if one was killed.

❧

There were giants in the earth in those days; and also after that, when the sons of God came in unto the daughters of men, and they bare children to them, the same became mighty men which were of old, men of renown.

—Genesis 6:4

Franklin Roosevelt and George C. Marshall were gods—Churchill, a god at a distance. As the stray vivid details of that period impressed themselves and settled into the collage of my memory, there seemed to be, to my boyish child's still local imagination, a unanimity of purpose, a forbearance and courtesy among the grown-ups. Or, in any case, there was clarity and fatalism, and a sense that all Americans were in this thing together. There was a distinct suppression of vanity (except in the cases of Generals George Patton and Douglas MacArthur, and theirs were battlefield vanities—ivory-handled pistols for Patton, grandiloquence for MacArthur—and therefore entertaining and forgivable). On the home front, the crisis of the world war elicited a pleasing self-effacement in people. Money was scarce and so were butter and gasoline and meat.

An idea of a unified and unambiguously virtuous America, as I perceived it in the house on Benning Road, in my parents' conversation, and in my uncles when they came home from Anzio and Normandy and the Battle of the Bulge, has never quite deserted me. Later generations would not understand it. Each of us comes from a different planet and is formed by the terrors or comforts of the crystallizing moments that the mind learns to regard as representative, as the truth of the world.

I think of a line from Evelyn Waugh's *Brideshead Revisited*: "These memories, which are my life—for we possess nothing certainly except the past—were always with me."

I had a higher opinion of America than my younger brothers and sisters did. They were members of the baby boom generation, born and raised when our parents were no longer so young and had acquired some money and lived a better life in general. My younger siblings mostly came of age in the 1960s, during the Vietnam era, which taught them a style of thinking about the country entirely different than the one that I had learned. I had gauzy protomemories of the war and the world in peril, of Iwo Jima and Normandy, and of great men, our hero fathers in battle; they had Lyndon Johnson and Robert McNamara and My Lai. Not heroes, but American grotesques. I trace our current troubles to that time—the youth of the boomers who are now old.

When I was not quite five years old, US district court judge Learned Hand delivered a speech in Central Park at a ceremony to swear in new citizens of the United States. It was May 1944, less than three weeks before the Normandy invasion. The speech became famous for a little while—*Life* magazine and the *New Yorker*, among others, printed the text, which contained sweet truths or bromides of an earlier America, the country that for three years had poured blood and treasure into the common purpose of defeating Hitler's Germany and the Japanese empire, the partners in evil.

Judge Hand began: "We are gathered here to affirm a faith, a faith in a common purpose, a common conviction, a common devotion." He invoked what he called "the spirit of liberty." He said it was "the spirit which is not too sure that it is right; the spirit of liberty is the spirit which seeks to understand the minds of other men and women; the spirit of liberty is the spirit which weighs their interest alongside its own without bias." In the late spring of 2020, to read the line "the spirit which is not too sure that it is right; the spirit of liberty is the spirit which seeks to understand the minds of other men and women" is to grow nostalgic and to lament the people that Americans have become.

Bless Judge Learned Hand. It is in such moments that one picks up a trace of the old music, and the trail of the hound, the bay horse and the turtle dove. The past is not inferior to the present. It is a different thing; being less immediate, it may also be less confusing. The past may come to seem, if you care about it and work at it, more fully developed—more mature, more intelligent, more finished, more accessible and consoling.

Or it may become more and more difficult and problematic. Judge Hand spoke about fourteen months before Hiroshima. Should Harry Truman have dropped that bomb? I thought so once; I have thought about it for years, and at different times have come down on different sides of the argument. No one will ever know the right answer. Another characteristic and irreconcilable difference.

We could have a long argument about all of this. The earth upon which I emerged on September 21, 1939 ("in a small private hospital in Philadelphia much favored by abortionists," as my father told me jauntily one day in the midsixties as we drove in his Mercedes toward Manhattan, on the parkway across from the Palisades on the Jersey side of the sparkling river) was doubtless very different from the one that greeted a newborn American in, let's say, Bill Clinton's second term (the salad days of Monica Lewinsky), or in the reign of frumious Donald Trump.

An American born at either of those moments will have first impressions of the country that are very different from the ones I formed. And imagine how the idea of America of those born in the spring of 2020 will be colored by the fact of having been born when a pandemic raged, the economy was in shambles, and cities all over the country were in flames, beset by racial angers and arsonists and looters and angry marchers.

Warsaw was in flames on the day I was born. A new era, that of World War II, had just begun. Now another era begins.

There is an American tradition—going much further back than Vietnam—of claiming that the past is a lie, and not worth fretting about anyway. But that does the past an injustice.

The past is a dream full of meanings. Money is a dream of the future. It has the energy of hope.

᷍

My mother looked a little like Ingrid Bergman. She became, briefly, a member of the Communist Party, but she quit after Stalin's Moscow Trials; when she did that, her Communist cell in Philadelphia declared her to be "an enemy of the people," a title that amused her and made her proud.

It was not unusual for people to be Communists in those days. In a memoir, the author Louis Auchincloss wrote: "Alfred Kazin, the great literary critic and my contemporary, told me once that in his West Side Manhattan boyhood everyone he knew had been a communist. I replied that in my East Side no one I knew had been." That was one of the intra-generational fault lines. My mother could have been Auchincloss's younger sister—or Kazin's. They were all roughly the same age, born in the time of Harding and Coolidge.

Auchincloss came from old New York money, from the Edith Wharton side of the society. He wrote:

> By the time of my father's generation (he was born in 1886), the
> sacredness of capital was an established creed, and even the

Vanderbilts (George of Biltmore always excepted) probably lived within their incomes. The work ethic applied to all. My father had two brothers-in-law born wealthy men who lost the bulk of their fortunes by insisting on managing their money themselves rather than leaving it to professionals. "Had they been beachcombers," Father used to say, "they'd be rich men today."

My parents had a glamorous but hectic idea of themselves and were ambitious and successful as journalists during the Truman administration. Years later, my mother's best friend (a Barnes of Philadelphia, called "Sister" Barnes) would marry John O'Hara, that gifted, surly Mick from the Pennsylvania coal region, who was, like my father, a doctor's son. She sequestered herself with O'Hara in Princeton, where he owned expensive cars—including a Rolls Royce and a Jaguar 3.8 sedan—and nursed his bruised pretensions and his resentment that he never got an honorary degree from Yale. Ernest Hemingway supposedly said that when O'Hara died, he'd go to Yale.

By the time O'Hara married Katharine, he had stopped drinking (his doctor had warned him it would kill him in six months if he didn't stop), but my mother said he remained the bastard he'd been before. Even cold sober, he still kept speakeasy hours. He wrote all night. He would wake up Katharine at midnight to make him a chicken sandwich. They played a game of Scrabble every afternoon.

Sister Barnes—Katharine Barnes Bryan O'Hara, a widow by this time—died when she crashed her Mercedes into a tree one winter night on her way home from a party in Princeton: a John O'Hara ending.

❧

My parents were often broke.

"Hughie, spot me a fin?" a guy would say to my father at the Press Club bar. I remember that man, a little Irishman in threadbare tweeds who worked for the *Denver Post*. He had wiry red hair, tensely curled, and bloodshot turquoise eyes, and leather patches on the elbows of his jacket. His hands trembled when he grasped the $5 bill. On a billboard in the lobby, the Press Club would post the names of members delinquent in their dues and bar bills, and it was a long list.

When my father called me, some ten or twelve years later, to tell me that the man had died, I hung up the phone, and, for a reason that I do not understand, I wept for half an hour—violent, heaving sobs. I had hardly known my father's friend Phil, but he represented a lost world: His death summoned up the accumulated emotion of the Great Depression, which made no sense, really. The Depression occurred before I was born.

My clearest memory of Phil was of a sunny noontime on Pennsylvania Avenue near the White House, by the Treasury, just across the way from the Riggs National Bank, a few blocks from the Press Club. Phil was keeping an eye on me for my father (I was five or six) and he held my hand as we crossed the avenue and asked me, in his sweet wisp of a brogue, for my opinion about something. Phil had a charming respect for children and he would talk to me as if I were just another drinking companion with whom to chatter.

The Depression conjured by his death was a phantom to me, but a haunting and heartbreaking psychic presence, nonetheless. My contemporaries will know what I am talking about.

Everyone was broke. Reporters were especially broke. (They never called themselves "journalists." They found the word ridiculous—hopelessly puffed up. "Reporter" would do. Or "newspaperman." Reporter described what you did—you *reported* the news. Newspaperman described what you were, even who you were: Someone maybe halfway between a plumber and a lawyer. Someone who wanted perhaps to be someone else—a novelist, a poet. Being a newspaperman was what you did to survive.)

The wages were lousy. The Newspaper Guild did its best. My father, when very young, worked hard to keep the Communists from taking over the Newspaper Guild at the *Inquirer*. He and his friends succeeded. He was a reporter for the *Inquirer* and later a Washington editor of the *Saturday Evening Post* in the days when it was an important magazine. Going to work for the magazine bumped him up a notch or two in respectability and salary.

It was the last of the golden age of magazines, before television arrived in earnest, and, of course, long before smartphones and social media. Magazines had immense importance and influence. The Alsop brothers, Stewart and Joseph, wrote for the *Post*. They were forces of public opinion. My father edited their pieces—articles were always called pieces then—and there was much talk at home about Joe and Stew, or "Stewie" as my mother called him, who were cousins of the Roosevelts (of both of the Roosevelts, since Eleanor and Franklin were themselves cousins), and, though obscurely, of Louis Auchincloss himself, whom records show to have been the fifteenth cousin, two times removed, of Teddy Roosevelt, via their common ancestor John of Gaunt. Money and blood and their generations are a dense American intertangling; raw money over the years subsiding often enough into mere gentility, or worse, into decay and poverty.

Auchincloss observed:

> One can still sympathize with those who feel the lack of an assured position in society. The secure person can enter a room of strangers with the confidence that he is just as good as any of them, no matter what title they may devise to describe themselves and be simply amused by any who deem themselves superior to him. If they exceed him in rank, legally, militarily, or however, that is because the political system calls for ranks and not because one person is entitled to look down on another. In any orderly society, rank has its function.

Auchincloss spoke for a world now gone.

Without the assurance of birth, the American might either recede and cower or brazen it out. If you want to brazen it out, like Donald Trump, you will not be content to be "just as good as any of them," but rather will want to be unquestionably superior, not by dint of birth but by reason of power or cunning or a ton of money. Outside the moneyed classes, you might succeed by talent, intelligence, and charm. The moneyed classes will always need to be amused.

Auchincloss became a lawyer, which was respectable, but he betrayed his social class by turning into a writer as well. My parents—very young and broke during the Depression, but good-looking, talented, and smart—in a sense had no social class at all. They belonged to the independent category of the bright and interesting.

The Depression was a ruthless leveler: Many of the rich grew suddenly poor and most of the poor grew poorer. Youth and beauty were assets then, almost as good as money in the bank. Style was a great thing, but style in Washington was different from style in New York, where people were sleeker and surer of themselves and laughed at Washington, if they bothered to think about Washington at all. A beautiful woman or a witty man would be relatively commonplace in New York, but in Washington would be unusual and almost suspect, like, let's say, a Westerner in Tokyo who upsets the Japanese by speaking their language too fluently.

In Washington, a mandate of small-town authenticity, not to say dullness, prevailed. Washington was the capital of the great democracy, and while candid ostentation was forgivable and maybe attractive—it passed as exuberant naïveté, a rejoicing in one's luck and one's oil wells—still one did not wish to put on airs or be too clever or too fashionable. Too rich was okay, because there was something endearingly oafish, endearingly American, about it. And besides, it was, after all, *money*. Money was like the famous exit visas in *Casablanca*—pieces of paper that opened all doors and rendered even the Nazis powerless.

My parents had an innocence that matched the bumptious innocence of the capital—the pageant of American just-folks trying to make themselves at home in the seat of power. Corruption, too, was allowable and taken for granted and winked at, as a way of fitting in and playing the game, of joining the pageant. There was in my parents a touch of Rudyard Kipling's Kim on the Grand Trunk Road. Their noses were pressed to the glass and they were ready for anything.

Norman Rockwell painted the covers for the *Saturday Evening Post*. One recognized in his American faces, as in many of the characters in Frank Capra's movies, a realignment of Americans' ideas of themselves in relation to money. He gave Americans an idea of themselves as a modestly middle-class people, homely but radiant with simple virtue, with wistfulness, hopefulness, and patience (for the Depression, for the war), but also, beneath the surface, somewhat smitten, marked by the unmistakable chill.

The Palestinian people refer to the year 1948, when the state of Israel was born, as the *nakba*, or the "great catastrophe." Serbians remember their defeat at the Battle of Kosovo in 1389 as if it happened six or eight months ago. The *nakba* and Kosovo became sanctified traumas. In the folklore of my parents' generation, that trauma was the Great Depression in America.

My mother wrote magazine articles and eventually a syndicated newspaper column about Washington society and politics. My parents knew how to play in the big leagues, but they made every rookie mistake. They had something of the quality of waifs dressing up and playing at being grown-ups in the capital, among the senators and congressmen whom they knew and sometimes ate and drank with. Washington was a smaller town then. One morning, my father was on the way to his office on Jackson Place, on Lafayette Square, when President Truman, out for his morning walk, called to him, "Hello, Hugh!"

Their experience in the Depression had given them the idea that planning ahead for much of anything (saving money, for example) was pointless in a world so prone to catastrophes. The life disasters of their youth, including the crash of 1929, the Great Depression, and World War II, were events both historical and intensely personal, and seemed to confirm their impression of the world's unreliability.

Over the years, they became to me, in memory, like characters in a novel that I had read a hundred times. They were so young that I loved them almost as one loves a brother and a sister—or even as one loves one's own children. The child of such parents is never quite a child and never quite the star of his own life.

My parents would have six children together, and my father would go on to have two more with his second wife and my mother would have a son with her second husband. There seemed something heedless in all this breeding, but who was I to object? My brothers and sisters and I went through storms together, and, in the midst of it all, there was ambiguity sometimes as to who was the adult and who was the child.

When my father died, he left each of us $34 in his will. Or was it $36? I cannot remember. We laughed but I don't think any of us minded. It was a great gag—and a commentary on the entire subject of money. Like a punch line. He had been a big cheese on Nelson Rockefeller's staff, and all he left any of us was $34. Everyone took his chances. Naked came I into the world, and $34 would pay for a modest dinner—for one person, without wine or tip. It's not clear that we have a right to expect more than that.

My mother and father came of age in the 1930s—if you allow that twenty-one and fifteen can be considered "of age." My father was the son of a central Pennsylvania country doctor who had eight children to feed. My grandfather—a lean, kindly, intelligent man with jug ears, who in his youth pitched semipro ball in Florida—ministered to farmers who, when he set a broken leg or delivered a child, could pay him only with a couple of chickens or a bushel of apples. In hard winters, neighbors sometimes left a box of groceries on the doctor's back porch so that his many children would have something to eat. My father learned to drive at age twelve by taking Dr. Morrow on house calls, ramming the Model T through snow drifts on remote farm roads—ramming, then backing up...and then ramming again.

My mother's father was wealthy in the 1920s, a manufacturer who rode around Pittsburgh in a chauffeur-driven Pierce-Arrow with enormous headlights. He had a mansion in Sewickly and carried a gold-headed cane and wrote bombastic Tennysonian poetry. He lost most of what he had in the way of money in the crash of 1929. To complete the humiliation, his wife had an affair with the gardener and then with the first violinist of the Pittsburgh Symphony Orchestra. Thereafter, he was a man bewildered and chastised by a world that he no longer understood.

These were the stories that emerged, in bits and pieces, from my parents' tellings, which had a tone of rue and satire and concealed hurt. That was the Depression note—the cello, the kazoo. If I were to choose one character who represented—incarnated—those years, I would name W. C. Fields. He is the madeleine. Watch Fields in *It's a Gift*, and that entire America returns.

The Great Depression took much from Americans in the way of money but compensated them in other coin—altered aesthetics, the rise of new politics, new ideas of the world. It toughened people. It conditioned them physically and mentally for World War II, made them leaner and more realistic than they had been in the comparatively heedless twenties. It made them both meaner and kinder. It warned them, rebuked their pride. It made them more ruthless.

It made them more interestingly sentimental. You saw that in the movies; there arose a genre of sentimentality. One side of my mother was an imitation of Shirley Temple, a tot in a storm, unstoppable. Shirley was usually orphaned or semiorphaned (temporarily separated from a parent's protection)—and the plot served as an allegory for the great national failure and parental betrayal (the Wall Street Crash, the collapse of capitalism) that had left the child—who was America herself—defenseless and naked to the elements.

The great American divide would be between the Common Man (Capra's people) and the heedless or sinister plutocrats. Recall the northbound bus in Capra's *It Happened One Night* (1934) plunging through the rainy dark (the Great Depression itself) and the passengers singing "The Daring Young Man on the Flying Trapeze," taking turns with the verses, as the millionaire's brat (Claudette Colbert, mistily elegant) sits in the back of the bus with Clark Gable. The spoiled rich girl is beginning to absorb the lessons that the journey will have to teach about the virtues of the ordinary and the meaninglessness of her father's money—"a lot of hooey," Clark Gable will tell her. The class of Americans missing from the bus that night were African Americans.

The Great Depression sobered America; the 1920s, under Prohibition, had been a notoriously alcoholic decade. In the new zeitgeist, Scott and Zelda Fitzgerald came to ruin. Utopian visions became fashionable; the dogmatic hallucinations of Marxism and Leninism and schismatic Trotskyism distracted the minds of intellectuals even as Franklin Roosevelt expanded and transformed the role of the American government.

&

Money and its lessons and a concomitant tendency to either prudence or folly may be genetically transmitted from father to son, mother to daughter. As I have said, it is an emotional, personal subject. When interpreted only by economists, accountants, or investment bankers, money loses its rich human texture—its pulsing actuality. At the same time, money is a novelistic phenomenon—a subject in some ways better understood by Dickens or Dreiser than by John Maynard Keynes. It is the realest and unrealest of subjects.

I have wondered whether it was the Depression of their youths that directed the narrative in which my father eventually became a top aide to an iconic moneybags, Nelson Rockefeller—signing on as his courtier and almost his ward—and in which my mother, after divorcing my father, married a member of the McCormick family of Chicago. Each of them found refuge, in other words, in a wealthy American dynasty.

4

In Mexico and Peru, the 16th-century Spanish were ferocious in the candor of their greed. It is true that Cortés brought Jesuits with him and asked Spain to send more missionaries, as he was devoted to the Virgin Mary and to making converts. Pizarro did not waste time on hypocrisy. He said: "I have not come for such reasons. I have come to take their gold away from them." And he did.

The desire for money superseded other passions, even the desire for sex. Greed trumped lust. I wonder if it always does.

The Spanish prospered in their search for gold at its sources. The English did not. V. S. Naipaul—whose grandparents emigrated from West India to Trinidad to work as indentured servants on the cocoa plantations—wrote about how he conducted research for his book *The Loss of El Dorado*:

> I used to go to the British Museum to read the Spanish documents
> about the region. . . . I was reading about the foolish search for El
> Dorado and the murderous interloping of the English hero Sir
> Walter Raleigh. In 1595 he raided Trinidad, killed all the Spaniards he
> could, and went up the Orinoco looking for El Dorado. He found
> nothing, but when he went back to England he said he had. He had
> a piece of gold and some sand to show. He said he had hacked the
> gold out of a cliff on the bank of the Orinoco.

There was a clarity of purpose—if not of information. *Geldwolfen*, "wolves of money," financed Henry Hudson's *Half Moon* farther north.

Hudson searched for China and he found Poughkeepsie. Like Rick Blaine who came to Casablanca for the waters, he was misinformed.

What if the Europeans landing in the New World had found it to be as desolate as Patagonia? Would they have given the New World a second glance, let alone bothered to stay and settle?

And if they had tried to put down roots in a Patagonia that could give them nothing back, how would the new land have evolved? Would they have called it a "City on a Hill"?

Jamestown became a warning parable—the American protofailure. There were some five hundred white, English colonists living there when the winter of 1609 began. By the time the spring came, only sixty remained, most of them sick or dying.

That was "the starving time." The crops failed because of drought. The water was brackish, the local Native Americans hostile and unwilling to trade for food. Harsh winter set in. Rather than risk venturing into the forest for firewood—the local people waited there in ambush—the colonists used their own houses for fuel. They ate cats, dogs, horses, and rats. Archaeologists found the remains of a girl of about fourteen, who seems to have been killed and butchered for meat.

What if this had happened to other settlements? What if America had not turned a profit? What would America be without its abundance— without its money? Would it have been a brawl—a Hobbesian horror?

Daniel Defoe approached such questions—basically, what is a civilization to be, and why? and how might you build it out of the materials at hand?—when he wrote *Robinson Crusoe*.

❧

My mother read the book to me when I was in bed with the measles. I ran a high temperature, which gave me fever dreams, and so the story as I first heard it had the quality of hallucinations sliding in and out of the conscious mind. There were overlapping "realities" in play: (1) the reality of my mother sitting beside the bed and reading a book aloud in my room in Washington in 1947; (2) the competing reality of the 1719 story that she read to me, in which Defoe conjured into life the fictional character of an

English mariner shipwrecked in a storm and left on a nameless Caribbean island in 1659; and (3) the reality created by those two dimensions as they fused in my feverish brain. No sooner had my mother read to me about the lone footprint that Crusoe discovered in the sand than I slipped into an agitated dream about it.

Defoe himself had the quality of a prototype, an American avant la lettre—a prolific literary genius and a marvel at mimicry and projection, who was also a hack and a noisy pamphleteer (he is known to have used 198 pen names), a secret agent from time to time (working for the government or the Earl of Oxford), and a political activist and dissenter who joined the Duke of Monmouth's plot against King James and somehow managed to survive its collapse. He'd seen the inside of a jail; he went in for dodgy, overelaborate business schemes. He lost a bundle when he purchased a swarm of civet cats with the thought of turning their musk into perfume.

On the other hand, he was an active, imaginative businessman and, late in life, the author of an exemplary guide called *The Compleat English Tradesman*. He started out in business as a hosier and flew high for a time on his wife's whopping dowry of what would amount to nearly $1 million in today's money, but he had a taste for risky projects and went bankrupt twice, was often in debtors' prison, and died, still scheming, at the age of seventy while hiding from his creditors.

Defoe would serve as both role model and cautionary tale—an introduction to the unstable ways and unreliable morals of money. With all of that, he was a major figure in English literature, pioneer of the novel.

In *Robinson Crusoe*, he wrote a prophetic masterpiece: an adventure story and a shopkeeper's myth of Adam. It proved to be a preliminary dream of America—a premonition of the country's middle-class soul, its racial dynamics, its class distinctions, and even of the lonely isolation of American individualism and material success.

The Life and Strange Surprizing Adventures of Robinson Crusoe, of York, Mariner: Who Lived Eight and Twenty Years, All Alone in an Un-Inhabited Island on the Coast of America became the blueprint of all these things, the American genome.

In 1912, James Joyce gave a lecture on Defoe at the Università Popolare in Trieste in which he interpreted *Crusoe* from a British perspective:

The true symbol of the British conquest is Robinson Crusoe, who, cast away on a desert island, in his pocket a knife and a pipe, becomes an architect, a carpenter, a knife grinder, an astronomer, a baker, a shipwright, a potter, a saddler, a farmer, a tailor, an umbrella-maker, and a clergyman. He is the true prototype of the British colonist, as Friday (the trusty savage who arrives on an unlucky day) is the symbol of the subject races. The whole Anglo-Saxon spirit is in Crusoe: the manly independence; the unconscious cruelty; the persistence; the slow yet efficient intelligence … the practical, well-balanced religiousness; the calculating taciturnity. Whoever rereads this simple, moving book in the light of subsequent history cannot help but fall under its prophetic spell.

The British colonist was the first American of the new settlement.

Crusoe's island, like America as the Europeans found it, is an improvisation—sometimes desperate and always a test of the cardinal American virtues of competence, sanity, and active self-interest. A couple of centuries later, D. H. Lawrence would deliver himself of the famous pronouncement that the essential American is "hard, isolate, stoic, and a killer." In *Crusoe*, Defoe made the same point in a nicer and more middle-class fashion. Crusoe's island home evolves and develops as America itself would evolve and develop—by trial and error, perseverance, and attention to detail.

☙

There is a spiritual kinship between *Robinson Crusoe* and John Bunyan's *Pilgrim's Progress*, another foundational document. The full title of Bunyan's wonderful book is *The Pilgrim's Progress from This World to That Which Is to Come, Delivered under the Similitude of a Dream. Wherein Is Discovered, the Manner of His Setting Out, His Dangerous Journey; and Safe Arrival at the Desired Countrey.*

Crusoe, for all its hardheaded and sometimes fussy realism, is also delivered under the similitude of a dream—it is one of the most persuasive and hypnotic hallucinations in literature: the record not only of

Crusoe's domestication and eventual mastery of his island over a period of twenty-eight years but also of his maturing moral sensibility. Thus, when he first encounters the visiting cannibals, he declares in outrage and abhorrence that he wants to slaughter them all. Over a period of time, he comes to a moral viewpoint that would give it credit with the most progressive of the 21st century's moral relativists. He allows that the cannibals' ways are their ways, thinking, *who am I to judge them and their habit of eating their enemies?* Crusoe is not the most likable character—neither was Daniel Defoe—and yet one is touched by his proto-American earnestness, his sifting and restless conscience.

Huck Finn says of *Pilgrim's Progress*: "[It] is about a man who left his family," and that is true of *Robinson Crusoe,* too. Both Christian and Crusoe have left behind the middle-class safety of their old life and ventured forth—just as the Pilgrims and those who came after them left behind their old lives in Europe. Bunyan's Christian is on a dangerous journey toward the Celestial City. Defoe's Crusoe goes to sea but has his journey interrupted by shipwreck somewhere in the Americas.

Both books record the soul's solitary struggle. Christian's dilemmas are spiritual—theological. Crusoe's problems are physical, practical. Christian has his Slough of Despond, and so does Crusoe.

One of Defoe's biographers, John Richetti, speaks of Crusoe as a kind of essayist: "[He] is defined by that effort at self-knowledge, but the effort by definition is continuous and unresolved."

I have entertained the notion that Americans themselves are essentially essayists—attempters—and that the country is an essay in history and ethics, a probing forward through time.

Defoe's gift of uncanny, almost documentary true-to-life recording of events—evident in *Robinson Crusoe, A Journal of the Plague Year,* and *Moll Flanders*—catches the confused dynamics, the false starts and contradictions, of life as it blunders on, improvising itself and getting regularly surprised. Fallibility makes for credibility. Life does not proceed neatly.

At the start of his island existence, the wreck of Crusoe's ship is just offshore. He swims out repeatedly to rescue the tools—the hatchets and gunpowder and guns, the two saws, axe, hammer, nails, grindstone, bread, iron cables, razors, scissors, knives and forks, pens and ink, paper, and much else—crucial odds and ends brought from the civilization from which he is now to be cut off. He is like the colonists who took with them the odds and ends of Europe—the tools and customs and values—to the New World, and with those, improvised the American society.

In one drawer, Crusoe

> found about thirty-six pounds value in money—some European coin, some Brazil, some pieces of eight, some gold, and some silver. I smiled to myself at the sight of this money: "O drug!" said I, aloud, "what art thou good for? Thou art not worth to me—no, not the taking off the ground; one of those knives is worth all this heap; I have no manner of use for thee—e'en remain where thou art, and go to the bottom as a creature whose life is not worth saving."

On second thought, he took the money along with him to the new home of his "robinsonade," his parable of survival and mastery.

The island is innocent of the need of money. For the moment, Crusoe represents humankind previous to money. Money is a medium of exchange and Crusoe has no one with whom to exchange anything: Whatever he makes is for himself. He plays the consolidated roles of sole proprietor, manufacturer, and consumer. That is the tragedy and the triumph of his solitude, although Crusoe, not having a tragic or melo-dramatic mind, does not think of it that way.

Instead he reckons his island life as a bookkeeper, tallying debits and credits, assets and liabilities. He makes a careful list of the pluses and minuses of his situation, enumerating the bad things in the left-hand column and the good things in the column on the right. He brings a shopkeeper's mind to his existential dilemma.

There's also the parable of race. The story foretells something of the racial dynamics to come in America. Friday appears and becomes a servant. Crusoe the European is master. The other people of color on the island are visiting cannibals. In time, race would become the most intensely emotional of American themes involving money and morals.

Daniel Defoe's ideas crossed over to the colonies and helped to shape them. In 1726, he published *The Compleat English Tradesman*, a subtle, systematic examination of the ethics and practices of merchants, entrepreneurs, and other businesspeople; a moral handbook for the nation of shopkeepers. The book is filled with shrewd, novelistic, moralistic anecdotes that Defoe acquired in his up-and-down career as a businessman, entrepreneurial visionary, and pioneer of economic journalism.

Defoe was one of the favorite writers of Benjamin Franklin, the spiritual founder of the American middle class, who imported him into American orthodoxy. Franklin softened and disarmed the harsh New England anxieties of soul. He codified, popularized, and secularized the ethics of small business, in effect diverting moral energies from their previous obsession with personal sin, from man's innate depravity and the soul's predestination. Following Defoe, Franklin framed the New World's dilemmas in a social-commercial context, grounding them above all in common sense, folk wisdom, and the spirit of humane, tolerant decency that more or less civilized the middle colonies (Pennsylvania and Maryland, for example). Here was the origin of the tendency—which is under threat now and perhaps departing—of the middling American temperament, the instinct to avoid extremes.

Franklin's adaptation of Christian morals—aligning habits of modest, everyday social responsibility (punctuality, honesty and fairness in business, enthusiasm for civic organizations) with self-interest—established a model (something like Cotton Mather's rowboat with its two oars driving a middle course to heaven) that legitimized and domesticated commercial moneymaking; attempted to discipline the more vicious and disrupting impulses of human nature (greed, cheating); and became in time the default mode of the American conscience.

One might draw a direct line across a century and a half of American evolution from Benjamin Franklin to Calvin Coolidge. The object of business was the making of money. That meant that enshrined in the beating heart of the New Jerusalem—the "exceptional" country that God founded and sponsored to be a paragon and a redeemer among the nations—would always be that fatal and necessary thing, the love of money. It was First Timothy's "root of all evil," which Americans sanctified.

In fact, it was the love of money that made the American heart beat as vigorously as it did. Here was the Golden Calf. Here was greed, one of the Seven Deadly Sins, which (whatever the higher ideals) would become the diverse nation's muse, its power animal and common denominator.

&

Hard times would alternate with El Dorado, the Klondike, Texas gushers. America is the journey from Jay Gatsby's mansion on Long Island to the Joads' migrant camp in California—and back again. The restlessly cycling ups and downs of America. The bitch goddess—success—would take turns with the nastier bitch—failure.

William "Billy" Crapo Durant founded General Motors and became the richest man in America. Then he went bankrupt in the Great Depression. He was so thoroughly cleaned out that to earn his living he opened up a bowling alley and snack bar in Flint, Michigan. He worked in the kitchen and slept in the back room and made plans to start his life over by opening a chain of thirty bowling alleys. Alas, it never happened. He died before he could make good on the scheme.

&

Robinson Crusoe lived twenty-eight years on his island. While he was away, his Brazilian plantation prospered handsomely, and when he returns to society, he finds himself a wealthy man. His fortune had accumulated on its own, under the stewardship of a friend, testimony to the strange autonomy of money, which bears some trace resemblance to the workings of grace, unmerited, in the earlier religious scheme of things.

Defoe gave to Crusoe the happy ending and the prosperity that he was not able to bestow upon himself.

5

It has been a strange, cold, and eerie May. There continues to be news of the mounting deaths from the coronavirus and of the immense financial devastation that the lockdown has caused. More than forty million jobs have disappeared.

By now, more than one hundred thousand Americans have died as a result of the pandemic. The country has been under quarantine, and in New York City, people locked up in their apartments week after week have started leaning out of their windows in the evening when hospital workers (nurses, doctors, technicians, and all the rest) get off work. The people cheer and bang pots and pans in gratitude.

Across the country, there have been cries to reopen the economy, because the losses in jobs and money have also destroyed lives, and there are angry demonstrations against the continued restrictions. Some of the demonstrators carry guns, even AR15 rifles.

Two devastations are in play—the disease itself and the stunned, paralyzed economy.

Then, on Memorial Day weekend in Minneapolis, a black man named George Floyd, forty-six years old, is arrested for allegedly passing a counterfeit $20 bill to pay for cigarettes at a convenience store. Four policemen subdue him (Floyd is 6′6″ tall and weighs 242 lbs.) and handcuff him and force him to lie face down on the pavement. One of the policemen puts his knee on Floyd's neck, and keeps it there for almost nine minutes. Floyd dies. His death—or, to be precise, the video of his death—sets the country on fire.

The coronavirus is forgotten. It is as if it never happened—except for the strange detail that people continue to wear masks. The national drama has changed. America has gone off on a different subject.

Demonstrations and riots break out in seventy-five cities. There is looting and arson and the burning of police cars. Police in Minneapolis abandon their precinct house when it is surrounded by a mob, who then ransack it when the cops are gone.

Black-clad provocateurs are at work among the ordinary looters. The proceedings, morally speaking, might be assigned a slot somewhere between Kristallnacht and the Boston Tea Party.

Many of the mass marches have been peaceful enough, fervent in their atmosphere; the lines of march have been swollen with young whites joining in such numbers that the demonstrations begin to take on a generational aspect—as if the white young mean to announce, *We have transcended race.*

❧

> *Bliss was it in that dawn to be alive,*
> *But to be young was very heaven.*

Wordsworth's lines in "The Prelude" referred to the French Revolution. They still sound foolish.

People watching the events in 2020 think of 1968, which is apt enough. Some venture that this is a "second Civil War." But in 1968, we also referred to what was going on at that time—the nightmare procession of assassinations, riots, and surprises—as a second Civil War. Perhaps, for clarity, the 2020 version should be called the "third Civil War."

On the other hand, the Civil War analogy being used seems too linear, too coherent—a cliché, even. The outbreak of protests and riots going on now, superimposed upon the pandemic, feels like a sudden event of physics or meteorology, a perfect storm of perfect storms, multilayered and interpenetrating and simultaneous.

The motives at work in the disturbances are mixed. So are the moods—a wind shear of psychologies and attitudes: hysteria, grief, anarchy, frolic, spectacle, revolution, a fest of selfies against a backdrop of flames. Anarchists out of Joseph Conrad's *Secret Agent* trade germs with angry blacks and young whites on skateboards or $2,000 bikes. The deadly serious and the deadly unserious appear side by side in the performance.

But a crowd on the march does anger better than it does grief. An angry crowd tends to become a mob, and a mob tends to smash windows, to loot and burn. Whatever blameless emotion may have prompted the protest in the first place gets corrupted into mere power. A mob will imitate the abuse of power that the demonstration was called to protest in the first place. But if the intention is to destroy American society, there is no problem. Everything is on track.

Diverse, pent-up energies break loose simultaneously—decades and even centuries of racial grievance; anxiety and frustration after months of pandemic and lockdown; and the sudden implosion of the economy. The country woke up to dégringolade, a tumbling down of the familiar world. The George Floyd disturbances become part of the avalanche.

The disturbances have been called forth by the deaths of Floyd and of Breonna Taylor and of Ahmaud Arbery—a cluster of atrocities. The disturbances are even about the incident between a white woman referred to as a "Karen" and a black man who is a Central Park birder. The birder asked the woman to put her dog on a leash, lest the animal disturb the thrushes, and she called the cops on him, saying a black man was threatening her life. The disturbances are about Donald Trump, too—paying him back in his own idiom, as his enemies believe—and about the irreconcilable differences between Trump's America and the one that is so passionate about making him and his deplorable kind go away and leave the country to people who think like themselves.

A friend from Minneapolis e-mailed: "The protesters are idealistic and their commitment to justice admirable, but many of them seem to share a generational sense of entitlement. When it's clear that one is right, immediate compliance must follow. Well, they're right about the raw deal blacks have, and the need for that to change, and that the cop barrel has a lot of bad apples, but they have no sense of the fragility of social order. The cautionary cushions of tradition, faith, patience, and the need to persuade others are missing from their consciousness. Something will snap, and the combination of pandemic, disruption by protest, and imminent joblessness for millions of workers will lead to a place hard to see precisely, but very probably very bad."

A quote from the Enlightenment slave owner Thomas Jefferson would resurface in the mind, as it did at the time of Watts and Newark and Detroit during the sixties: "I tremble for my country when I reflect that God is just, that his justice cannot sleep forever."

The bravest people I knew when I was young were the civil rights workers in the South—the generation of Michael Schwerner, James Chaney, and Andrew Goodman, the trio murdered as they tried to register black citizens to vote in Neshoba County, Mississippi, in the summer of 1964. They were the Freedom Riders, clubbed bloody and senseless in Anniston and Birmingham, Alabama. They were the ones (John Lewis and Hosea Williams and the rest) who tried to cross the Alabama River on the Edmund Pettus Bridge on Bloody Sunday, 1965.

I think of them—of their physical courage and moral discipline, of the *satyagraha* (nonviolence) that they had learned from Gandhi and from King—as I watch the spectacle in the late spring of 2020. It was an entirely different country then, of course, but it was, in some respects, the same.

The killing of George Floyd in Minneapolis is the sort of thing that took place frequently in that earlier America. But there were no cell phone cameras with which onlookers might record such deeds in those days, and no Internet and social media that might, in an almost metaphysical flash, project upon millions of the world's screens the spectacle of a black man's slow dying on the pavement under the knee of a white policeman.

In Providence, the violence after George Floyd's death was as bad as in other cities. After one night's riots, Rhode Island's governor, Gina Raimondo, held a news conference in front of a shuttered mall. "What we saw last night," she said, "was an organized attack on our community at a time we are already vulnerable."

"They weren't even pretending to protest. They showed up in the middle of the night, angry, with crowbars and flares and buckets of gasoline with one purpose: to set our city on fire and hurt people."

John Brown was an eminently respectable and civilized man in his own time and his own world, a leader of the family who helped to found the city of Providence. He played a role in the origin of the American colonists' rebellion against the British crown. It was Brown who organized the Gaspee Affair in 1772—a middle-of-the-night attack upon a British revenue ship that had been sent to interdict the vigorous coastal smuggling trade in which the Browns, among other prominent merchant families, engaged. He and his co-conspirators wounded the British captain and burned his ship. Everyone knew Brown was behind the deed, but his fellow citizens protected him from British investigators who, if they had known the truth, might have ruined him and his family.

John Brown was one of the leading merchant patriots whose quarrel with the mother country boiled down to matters of money. The Brown family—the brothers John, Joseph, Nicholas, and Moses, who were the fifth generation of Browns in the New World—founded the school that became Brown University. John and Moses started one of America's first banks. Moses, in the words of the brothers' biographer, Charles Rappleye, "established on the shores of the Blackstone River the first mechanized cotton mill on this side of the Atlantic, allowing American weavers to compete on equal footing with England and inaugurating the Industrial Revolution."

The brothers were active and important in creating the country—representative Americans.

Rappleye writes, "Each emerges as an American archetype—Moses as the social reformer, driven by conscience and dedicated to an enlightened sense of justice; John as the unfettered capitalist, possessed of the prerogatives of profit and defiant of any effort to constrain his will."

The conflict between John and Moses Brown—an early study in the relationship of America's God and Mammon—first crystallized in the 1764 voyage of their slave ship *Sally*, of which I shall tell in a moment.

"Their religion is trade and their god is gain," said the governor of Rhode Island, John Collins. He was referring to the flourishing merchant class of Newport and to one great source of their "gain"—the African slave trade. By the time of the French and Indian War, fully 70 percent of the American ships engaged in the triangle slave trade sailed out of Newport, on vessels carrying rum as they headed east to the African Coast, carrying slaves as they traveled westward from Africa to the slave markets of the Caribbean or to ports like Savannah or Charleston, and carrying sugar and molasses as they sailed north on their way back to Rhode Island. Out of that last cargo, Newport had learned how to make superb high-octane rum that was a prime medium of exchange on the African coast.

The merchant Stephen Hopkins, another leader of Providence, emphasized the crucial role played by rum and slaves in the fortunes of the colony:

> This little colony...has annually sent about eighteen sail of vessels to the [African] coast, which have carried about eighteen hundred hogsheads of rum, together with a small quantity of provisions and some other articles, which have been sold for slaves, gold dust, elephants' teeth, camwood, etc. The slaves have been sold in the English islands [of the Caribbean], in Carolina and Virginia, for bills of exchange...and by this trade alone, remittances have been made from this colony to Great Britain, to the value of about 40,000 pounds yearly.... From this deduction of the course of our trade, which is founded in exact truth, it appears that the whole trading stock of this colony, in its beginning, progress and end, is uniformly directed to the payment of the debt contracted by the import of British goods; and it also clearly appears, that without this trade, it would have been and always will be, utterly impossible for the inhabitants of this colony to subsist themselves, or to pay for any considerable quantity of British goods.

Slavery and the slave trade, here explained and accepted as an economic necessity, became an evil that blighted the God-Mammon relationship in the deeper dynamics of the country's moral life. It is impossible to write about that history without referring to God—and to sin. The most influential anti-slavery document of the 19th century, *Uncle Tom's Cabin,* is an essentially religious text: melodramatic hagiography. Every syllable of *The Battle Hymn of the Republic* proclaims the connection: "As He died to make men holy, let us die to make men free."

The African slave trade was business at its most primitive—the barter of rum or other things (trinkets, firearms, bolts of cloth) for people kidnapped in the African interior and marched in coffles to the coast. Slavery goes back to ancient times in most parts of the world, of course; so do all of the world's other taboos and depravities. Most experience with slavery prior to the Europeans' arrival in Africa did not involve such absolute distinctions of skin color, such mass systematic harvesting of slaves, the transportation of slaves across the ocean to another continent, or their organization in totalitarian agricultural operations—huge sugar or rice plantations, for example. Anyway, no quantity of historical precedent could have, for very long, made slavery seem right or moral in an honest Christian's mind.

Still, Southern ministers exerted themselves to portray slavery as a vaguely benevolent institution, almost until the moment that General Sherman arrived to burn the plantations. The slave trader and slave owner offered a protoracist rationale as the crux:

> The black African is not my "neighbor." He is a different color; he
> has different hair and does not wear shoes or trousers. He comes
> from a lower civilization—even from a different stage of evolution
> [said the slave owner]. When Christ spoke of "thy neighbor," he
> referred to a like creature, fashioned in the image of God, co-equal in
> the sight of God. The African is a creature unlike the white European
> or the white European-American in body and brain.

The African is Other—outside the pale of those systems of instinct and morals and courtesies that oblige people to be decent to one another and, if you insist, to "love" one another, in Christ's somewhat pushing formulation.

So if the African black could be taken up on the Guinea Coast; purchased for so many hogsheads of rum; shackled and stripped of name and identity (except for his generic and damning blackness, which is all the identification he would need where he was going, except perhaps for some fanciful Roman name like "Cato" or "Caesar"—a mocking reference to the galactic distance between the African and the noble Roman whose name was ridiculously fastened upon him, as upon a dog); locked in the hold behind the barracoon; borne gasping and half-dead across the ocean to a slave market in St. John or Kingston or Santo Domingo or Newport or Baltimore or Savannah or New Orleans; and sold for hard cash—if these things could happen, then presumably the slave ship captain and his supercargo, the slave trader, the slave owner, the master and the mistress, the other white folk about the plantation and the community, and the minister who preached to them on Sundays, all of them would be able to abet one another in the conceit that the African slave is not a quite human being but is something else, that he exists in some other category, and that he is not, in any case, covered in the same way that white people are covered by God's law and Christ's love—not really. Let that suffice on the theological side. But in any case, proslavery apologists would continue, the African thus removed from his homeland was better off in American slavery, serving white men across the water, than he was remaining at home at the mercy of a regime even more barbaric.

So the sinners would tell themselves that their immense sin was not a sin—not really, not quite. In speeches to buck up his fellow citizens of the Confederacy, Jefferson Davis went on and on about how they were fighting the Civil War in the cause of "freedom" (from Yankee tyranny)—to avoid being "enslaved" by Abraham Lincoln. Davis's vocabulary was Orwellian long before George Orwell was born.

Such attitudes—they were not really arguments but pigeon-breasted 19th-century rhetoric—sought to make the stupendous violation seem blameless and even benevolent. John Brown of Providence told his brother Moses that he would drop the slaving business in a second if it could be proved to him that the business was wrong. But he did not believe it to be wrong. John Brown stopped just sort of saying that by enslaving black Africans, white people did them a favor.

A corollary of the John Brown rationale would ripen later on: that slavery was the price Africans had to pay for admission to the advanced white civilization. The idea suggested that whatever the cruelties and injustices of slavery, of the subsequent Jim Crow discrimination, and of blacks' second-class citizenship in the whites' society, all of that represented a necessary readjustment and correction of evolutionary misalignments. Slavery was a sort of initiation—an apprenticeship in superior white ways and white culture. Slavery amounted to an involuntary education. African blacks did not ask to be enrolled in the program, but never mind. Booker T. Washington, whom we shall visit a little later, worked variations on the theme.

White Christians reassured themselves, as well, that blacks' abjectness (their poverty, ignorance, involuntary servitude) was a signal of God's disapproval of them, or sure proof of his indifference to their fate. If God had permitted blacks to be reduced to the lowest of human conditions, he could not have a very high opinion of them—and if that was God's thinking on the matter, why should the white man disagree? It was not a matter about which white people wished to think very hard, but by enslaving Africans, they took sidelong comfort in the thought that they were pretty much reaffirming God's verdict on black people.

Slavery was about theology and about money simultaneously. Part of the old poison, much dissipated now, was a notion that the black man may be a sort of devil, or that something of Satan had rubbed off on him.

In a reciprocal way, blacks have often believed—and asserted—that the white man is a devil. The Nation of Islam's newspaper *Muhammad Speaks* routinely referred to the "blue-eyed, white devil slave master."

Whites and blacks in America have each taken the other to be a devil and have each thought and spoken about the other in vividly superstitious (and, incidentally, racist) terms that reflect the traumatic relations between the two from the beginning. Whites and blacks have been each other's evil twin, each other's antiself.

The manifest of the hundred-ton brigantine *Sally*—master Esek Hopkins, departing Newport on September 11, 1764, bound for the Windward Coast of Africa—listed a cargo of 1,800 bunches of onions, thirty boxes of spermaceti candles, forty barrels of flour, fifty-one loaves of sugar, and other supplies and trade goods. The most important item was 17,274 gallons of rum, to be traded for slaves.

In their instructions, *Sally*'s owners—the Brown brothers, of Nicholas

Brown & Co.—asked Captain Hopkins to set aside "four likely young slaves," aged about fifteen years, for the Brown family's own use back in Providence. There was a provision for the captain's standard commission of four slaves for every 104 he delivered alive; Hopkins—who in later years would become the first commodore of the United States Navy—was also offered the "privilege" of ten slaves to sell on his own account.

The four Brown brothers were embarked upon their first venture in the trans-Atlantic slave trade. It turned into a fiasco. More than half the slaves that Captain Hopkins had painstakingly acquired, in ones or twos or threes, in difficult, complicated trading on the Gambia shore, died in transit. There was a slave revolt in mid-ocean, and Hopkins opened fire upon the Africans with musket and swivel gun. Several died. The deck ran with blood. *Sally* plunged on. More slaves committed suicide or perished from weakness and despair. Even after the brig made it to Antigua, slaves continued to die.

The Africans who survived, weak and sick, fetched very low prices. Captain Hopkins limped home to Providence.

After that experience, the quiet, reflective Moses Brown withdrew from the slave trade. He became a Quaker and an abolitionist and devoted years to working against the iniquitous business. John Brown—a gambler and a plunger—continued in the slave trade down the years. Even though the brothers clashed repeatedly on fundamental principles—John was once tried in court for violating an anti-slavery statute that Moses had helped to usher into law—their tribal solidarity was stronger than their moral differences and the brothers remained loyal and loving to each other.

6

Some years ago, the wooden shed that was our farm's icehouse in the 19th century fell apart, and so we cleared the wreckage away and discovered underneath a foundation made of big rough stones arranged like the walls of a canyon or a quarry. It was in that walled, rock-lined pit that the ice had been stored, smothered in sawdust. We turned the boxy pit into a small pond that is a favorite of local frogs. We planted lilacs beside it, and a peach tree that is just now coming into fruit. The birds and squirrels and other creatures get most of the peaches, but the tree gives comfortable, dappling shade on a summer morning. I sit there now, watching the sun come up over the ridge, pouring as it rises a slow, pure light of early June across the field.

All over the country, there have been days and nights of demonstrations against the police and police brutality and even against the very idea of police. Yesterday in Minneapolis, where the present trouble started, the City Council voted to dismantle the city's police department.

The eruption is mostly, deeper down, against Donald Trump and the mentality of Trump's America. The combination of Trump's provocations and the coronavirus have conjured a state of emergency in the media and in the minds of millions. All previous rules seem to have been suspended or abolished and anything has become possible, even, for the moment, a world without police.

Over the weekend, the *Philadelphia Inquirer* fired its white editor because the newspaper had printed a headline that read, "Buildings Matter, Too." The *New York Times* forced out the white editor of its opinion pages because he had allowed to be printed an op-ed piece by a conservative white senator, Tom Cotton of Arkansas, advising that federal troops should be called in to control the rioting and arson in American cities. In Washington, DC, the black mayor, Muriel Bowser, arranged to have the slogan "BLACK LIVES MATTER" painted in enormous yellow letters on the pavement along Sixteenth Street NW, near the White House. She put up signs naming that stretch of street Black Lives Matter Plaza.

It happens this way each time—the "all changed, changed utterly" moment, when, as W. B. Yeats wrote, "The best lack all conviction and the worst are full of passionate intensity." He was writing about the Easter Rising, a rebellion by the Irish against British rule that took place in 1916. The lines of his poem would become an editorial writer's cliché. In 2020, everyone has too many uncompromising convictions, too many fears. There is intoxication everywhere—the certitude of impulse and social media; I think of the French town that ate the bread that harbored a fungus that caused all of the people of the town to lose their minds at the same time. So many of the civilized have become believers, and their eyes are enameled, glazed over, and shine with virtue—delighted and relieved to have discovered a story, and a role, in which they can believe. They stopped believing in their country, or in American Virtue, a good long time ago, and so here, with one-fifth of the 21st century already squandered, they have leapt out of the pandemic lockdown to give themselves over to the new story that is also a continuation of the country's oldest.

7

The tale of Thomas Jefferson and Sally Hemings touches the emotions of American money as intimately and mysteriously as any.

Sally Hemings was Jefferson's slave, his property—and also, one must think, in one way or another, his love. She was his chattel and the companion of his bed for thirty-odd years and the mother of his children, who were also born his slaves. She was the half-sister of his dead wife, Martha Wayles Jefferson, whose father, John Wayles, a lawyer and slave trader, had begotten Sally with Elizabeth, a slave woman on his plantation. It goes without saying that John was white and Elizabeth was black.

Jefferson and Hemings began their sexual relationship when he was the American minister to Paris, a forty-six-year-old white man, and she was a sixteen-year-old servant girl. They would remain together, as master and slave and not entirely invisible lovers—is that the word?—whose relationship would provoke gossip, political scandal, and abuse ("Dusky Sally" and so on) until his famously timed death on July 4, 1826. Jefferson died on the same day as John Adams, exactly fifty years after the Declaration of Independence that had started it all. It was young Thomas Jefferson who wrote the sacred American words "We hold these truths to be self-evident, that all men are created equal."

Thomas Jefferson died broke. His money was gone. He owed more than $107,000 to his creditors. Much of his debt had been accrued by his late father-in-law, John Wayles, and had been passed on to Jefferson through the fortune—and the inherited financial obligations—that Jefferson's wife, Martha, had brought to the marriage. Debt, sometimes massive, was a way of life among the Virginia planters, with their vast estates and considerable overhead and income that fluctuated according to the vagaries of weather and the market in tobacco. And, in any case, Jefferson was a man of extravagant tastes—in French wines, in rare books, and in much else. The soil of Albemarle County, Virginia, was played out; plenty of farming families had moved on, farther west, to Kentucky or Ohio. Tobacco had exhausted the farmland. It was a crop as hard on the soil that grew it as it was on the lungs that smoked it.

Slaves were the family's living assets. The extensive Hemings family had been with the Jefferson, Wayles, and Randolph families for decades. With Jefferson's death, Martha Jefferson Randolph, the president's daughter, was obliged to sell Monticello and all its contents. A grand sale was announced in the newspapers and commenced on January 15, 1827. All of the slaves except five, all the household furnishings, farm animals, memorabilia, engravings, grain, farm equipment—everything except Jefferson's personal effects—would be auctioned off. If family members wanted to keep one item or another, they would have to pay for it. The only records of the sale would be letters of family members describing what they had acquired, along with some odd receipts for money still owed to Mrs. Randolph for various purchases.

The *Niles Weekly Register* reported that the executors raised $12,840 to pay the interest on the debt and $35,000 toward the principal. A few years later, the executors finally found a buyer for Monticello itself. He was James Turner Barclay, who ran an apothecary shop in Charlottesville. He purchased Monticello and its 552 acres for $7,500. He had the idea of developing the grounds to raise silkworms. He and his wife seem to have destroyed many of Jefferson's rare-specimen plantings in order to put in mulberry trees.

The financial dilemma that led to the selling of Monticello, its furniture, and slaves sounded like the same one that the merchant Stephen Hopkins set forth in Providence when he explained why the slave trade was necessary to keep Rhode Island afloat: Slavery and the slave trade were an essential part of an entire economic system, and Mammon had to be paid.

What became of Sally Hemings after Jefferson's death? As the historian Annette Gordon-Reed explains at the end of her 2008 work, *The Hemingses of Monticello*:

> After Jefferson's death Sally Hemings and her sons went to live in
> a rented house on Main Street in Charlottesville, not far from her sis-
> ter Mary. Later her sons would buy their own homes, and she would
> live with her son Madison. Word spread of her informal emancipa-
> tion, for she and her sons were listed in the 1830 census as free white
> people, even though it is inconceivable that the census taker did not
> know who she was. Her honorary whiteness did not last, however.
> Three years later, in a special census of 1833, conducted to count the
> free blacks in the community for purposes of determining which of
> them wanted to be resettled in Africa, Hemings described herself
> as a free mulatto who had lived in Charlottesville since 1826. She
> and her sons declined to return to Africa. They continued to live in
> downtown Charlottesville... until her death in the 1830s.... [A]s the
> years passed, the choices the children of Sally Hemings made would
> separate their lives forever. Three would live in the white world, and
> one would remain in the black world.

The story of Tom and Sally had the quality of a Harlequin Romance that strayed into history—a tabloid scandal and an American racial epic, touching and mysterious.

It is difficult, even at this remove, to know exactly what to make of Thomas Jefferson. Of the two—if you think of them in a Harlequin Romance way, as "a couple"—Sally seems somehow to have been the more attractive. Jefferson was the master of Monticello, with its Palladian clarities, and in regard to Sally and the other Hemingses (such as her older brother James, Jefferson's sometime body servant), he displayed also a certain moral evasiveness and even laziness that seem to the 21st-century mind to have been heartless and negligent but also of its time. On the other hand, Jefferson was an exact, methodical man, and perhaps his behavior should not be interpreted as callous negligence but rather as a deliberate strategy designed to protect Sally and her family from many savage possibilities. Relationships between slave owners and slave women such as Sally Hemings were common and often brutal. Marriage was impossible. Jefferson never seems to have mistreated Sally (except, of course, by holding her in slavery); on the contrary, he lavished a good deal of special attention on her, as when, in Paris, he spent a lot of money on having her treated by a doctor who had attended the King of France.

But she was his property and his slave. One must avoid anachronism. They belonged to their time and its ways. Gordon-Reed's book brilliantly explores the nuances of servitude, dependence, fear, loyalty, and other factors that were inherent in the dynamics of master and slave.

Did they love each other? That's an anachronistic, sentimental question—probably absurd. But on the other hand, they must have. They were together for well over thirty years. They had children together. And yet, the children, who after all looked a good deal like the third president of the United States, were slaves. As was their mother. Slavery does not speak of love, although, on the other hand, the human heart finds ways to make unexpected exceptions.

The relationship between the slave owner and the slave and that between husband and wife in white marriage at the time perhaps have their assonance, their superficial or tendentious points of comparison, in the sense that both an enslaved black and a white wife were circumscribed by the master's or the husband's will. But one would not claim, preposterously, that Abigail Adams or Martha Washington was as much a slave as Sally Hemings was.

Nullification would become an important American word—the claim that a state ought to be able to judge whether a particular federal law should be null and void within that state's borders. The Civil War would be fought on that essential point.

It applied in another sense: Slavery attempted the nullification of the enslaved. The story of blacks in America for four hundred years would be their struggle to survive and undo that nullification.

The story of Thomas Jefferson and Sally Hemings is fascinating and maddening and touching because it occurred in dangerous, conjectural territory that lay between the lawful and the forbidden, between the public and private, between the historic and the intimate, between power and powerlessness—between nullification and fulfillment.

Who knows if they were happy with each other, in their fashion, at Monticello, where Jefferson's writ was absolute, where he was Prospero on his island?

When Sally was a girl, with a distinguished middle-aged lover, she had a choice whether to remain in Paris, where she was free and protected by French laws against slavery, or to return with Jefferson to Virginia, where she would be a slave again and liable, among other things, to be sold at the whim of her master. She was still just a girl in her teens when she made her decision.

She chose to return to Virginia with Jefferson, and to slavery—and what is one to say in the face of such a choice? Was her decision thoughtless or profound? Is it possible that that choice—to return to Virginia—meant that her condition thereafter might be described as voluntary servitude? Or was she too young to make such a decision?

It is interesting to imagine the life that Hemings might have had in France if she had stayed behind. She might have set up a business, a shop of some kind, for example, and might have married happily and had children who were not—as hers would be in Virginia—slaves who would be worth so many hundreds of dollars on the American market: slaves whose dollar value would be considerably greater if the buyers knew that the blood of Thomas Jefferson flowed in their veins. What would a plantation owner pay for a boy who was, after all, half a Thomas Jefferson?

Or what if Jefferson, after the presidency, had sold Monticello, and, with Sally, moved the household permanently to France, where they would become expatriates, and where they might marry, and where she and their children would be free?

But the realities neither of American history nor of Thomas Jefferson himself were that sentimental.

8

The book is called *The Last Negroes at Harvard: The Class of 1963 and the 18 Young Men Who Changed Harvard Forever*.

Its author, Kent Garrett, born in Brooklyn's Fort Greene projects, was one of those eighteen young men. So was my friend Travis Williams. Kent called them "the last Negroes at Harvard" because, presently, the term "Negro" would be retired in favor of "black" and later, "African American." I, too, was a member of the class of '63. I am white.

In the book, I am mentioned here and there as a bit player in Travis's story. Kent published our headshots from Harvard's *Freshman Register* of 1959—two earnest young men, in horn-rimmed glasses, wearing jackets and ties, our hair cropped short.

Two years after we graduated, Watts erupted. "Long hot summers" became routine. I went to work as a writer for *TIME*; my first cover story for the magazine was about the Detroit riots of 1967. The Silent Generation yielded to the Vietnam Generation. Travis became a reporter for *Life*. We would meet after work for drinks at La Fonda del Sol on the first floor of the Time & Life Building in Rockefeller Center.

It is now a long, complicated lifetime later. Kent and his partner and coauthor, Jeanne Ellsworth, came to my farm to interview me for their book. We spent an afternoon talking about our class and Harvard and Travis—and Travis's death. In the spring of 1968, he died at twenty-seven of a cerebral hemorrhage at St. Vincent's Hospital in Greenwich Village. Our classmate John Woodford, one of the eighteen, my then-wife, and I flew to Durham, North Carolina, for the funeral.

Travis, a National Merit scholar, was brilliant, courageous, funny, full of promise. He drank too much. It was alcohol—aggravating his high blood pressure, taking advantage of a weakness in his blood vessels, which seems to be a problem especially affecting blacks—that killed him. We speculated that other things as well were eating at him. After he died, I remembered what he had told me about his father, a barber from Durham, who had gone to France to fight in World War I, and, like so many other black soldiers, returned home to the same-old Jim Crow South. Travis said his father hated white people. Travis didn't. He had many white friends.

In my conversation with Kent at the farm, the bitter story of race was the implicit background of our harmless memories of Harvard—the parietal hours, the roast beef sandwiches from Elsie's, Joan Baez singing at the club on Mount Auburn Street.

As we talked about Travis, I thought: Look, Travis was my best friend for nine years. Race had nothing to do with it. I was defensive. I knew that race had always been there.

Kent sent me a signed copy of *Last Negroes*. I flipped through it—looking first, of course, for myself. The book includes accounts of some of the hell-raising Travis and I did back then—like getting loaded on Jim Beam bourbon one winter night while sitting in the middle of the frozen Charles River, then going back to Dunster House to fire my .22 rifle into the logs in the fireplace.

The Last Negroes at Harvard is a wary, complicated, handsomely judicious book smoldering with a racial grievance that is both soothed and exacerbated by the condescension and privilege that Harvard lavished on the author and the seventeen other "Negroes." They were welcomed into Harvard's opulent, historic sanctuary around the same time James Meredith risked his life to integrate "Ole Miss," Medgar Evers was assassinated in Jackson, Mississippi, and Martin Luther King Jr. wrote his "Letter from Birmingham Jail." In the surreal neverland of Harvard, one of Kent's roommates in Eliot House was David Rockefeller. Another Eliot House resident was the Unabomber, Ted Kaczynski. What a country.

Kent and I did not know each other in those days. I was friendly with John Woodford, who was Travis's freshman roommate, the son of a doctor in Benton Harbor, Michigan. John and I are still friends. He wrote his honors thesis on *What Maisie Knew*, a novel by Henry James, and I did mine on the work of Vladimir Nabokov. Later, when the sixties got serious, John became the editor of *Muhammad Speaks*, the Nation of Islam's newspaper, which, as I have mentioned, would refer routinely to the "blue-eyed white devil slave master." I did not take it personally.

As I sat with Kent and Jeanne that afternoon at the farm, I was irritated that those two subjects—race and friendship—were assumed to be at odds with each other. I thought of W. E. B. Du Bois's formulation of the "double consciousness": "One ever feels his two-ness—an American, a Negro; two souls, two thoughts, two unreconciled strivings; two warring ideals in one dark body, whose dogged strength alone keeps it from being torn asunder."

John's transition from the novels of Henry James to the editorship of *Muhammad Speaks* became my favorite example of the terrific cultural whiplash of the double consciousness.

Was it the double consciousness that killed Travis? Maybe. A part of him never got over his father's rage, and of course he had angers and grievances of his own.

But the Du Bois idea seems a little too metaphysical and pat. Travis was indignant and anarchic, not tormented. I prefer to think that he died because he was reckless and young and full of life and, until the blood vessel burst in his brain, amazingly lucky. He was as strong as an ox and, for that reason, he overestimated his capacity to get away with just about anything. He thought he would live forever, not die at twenty-seven. His death, if anything, confirmed his idea of life as something absurd and therefore hilarious. He was no one's victim but his own. He was a man.

9

In Henry James's novels, published during the Gilded Age and after, the source of family money was kept decorously obscure, as if the characters (and even the author himself) had transcended the vulgarities of trade and manufacture, and risen, as who should say, to a finer elevation. The author after all was raised on money inherited from his grandfather's businesses in Albany; his father, Henry James Sr., had sufficient wealth to devote his life to writing unreadable treatises on Swedenborg and leading the family on restless itineraries of self-improvement. (The father's Swedenborg obsession led his son William James to design, as a gift for him, a book plate that showed a man beating a dead horse.)

In contrast to Henry James's novels, the relentlessly masculine *Moby Dick* (1851) tells the reader precisely how the money was made. The effect is metaphysical and gruesome: raw America. Whalers sail out from Nantucket and scour the seven seas, and hunt whales down and slaughter them. They bring a noble monster alongside and, surrounded by blood-maddened sharks, strip off the creature's blubber in hunks—mattresses of whale flesh—and lift it on deck with windlasses. They sever the head, savage the carcass for spare parts (sawing up the jawbone, for example), and at last cut loose the remnants and let them sink in a boil of sharks. They cook the blubber down, barrel it, and lower it into the hold, and after a cruise of two or three years, haul it home and turn it into fuel for lamps and bones for corsets. This is capitalism as alchemy. They have turned God's great creature into money. The American question would always be whether the lost nobility could ever be restored, and, if so, how. Or was it—is it—the necessary blood sacrifice?

Moby Dick is many things, among them a tremendous soliloquy on money and morals and the American mind. American egotism aspires to theology; revenge is inflated to cosmology, and the mere money-making business of whaling turns into biblical or Shakespearean drama. The first mate, Starbuck, represents the principle of sanity in business: the Chamber of Commerce, the Rotary Club, the Benjamin Franklin principle. Captain Ahab is the American mind gone back to fanaticism, to a primitive mania previous to all shopkeeping. Ahab casts away the second of Cotton Mather's oars. He resigns from Rotary and Kiwanis. He abandons the *Pequod*'s proper business and circles the globe in profitless search for one white whale. The power of whiteness and the power of blackness—the cosmic moral either-or—refer also to the struggle between money and virtue, venality and innocence. Ahab nails a gold doubloon to the mast. Melville contemplates some immense desecration. Who is the sinner? Ahab himself? Bildad and Peleg, the capitalist Quakers who own the *Pequod*? The consumers of the lamp fuel and corset stays? Humanity? The whale? America?

The lessons remain as enigmatic as those of the Book of Job, another treatise on the mysteries of wealth, providence, and virtue: *Where is wisdom to be found, and where is the place of understanding?* Both Job and *Moby Dick* posit the sardonic God. In the opening passage of Job, God and Satan talk like mafiosi: "Where ya been?" "Oh, I been around, here and there."...

The Book of Job is an important and even a pivotal American document because it deals in extremes of success and failure as they play out under the gaze of a moody Providence that might make bets with Satan on a whim. America has always tried to think of itself as Job *without* the catastrophes. That was the idea of the country: to be Job without the catastrophes, God's prospering favorite in the land of Uz.

In a somewhat analogous way, America has sought, from time to time in the years after 1945, to be Christ without the crucifixion—a redeemer nation unto the world, but without the necessity of sacrifice. That was not true of the Civil War, of course: Abraham Lincoln was the sacrificed Christ in that drama.

10

The country invents and reinvents itself.

Ulysses Grant, a West Point graduate, fought handsomely in the Mexican-American War, even though he disapproved of it. But afterward, in the 1850s, he found himself selling firewood to support his family. Old friends crossed to the other side of the street when they saw him in St. Louis or Galena, Illinois, in fear that he would try to borrow money from them.

Grant's was an unexpected American life, mysteriously comprehensive in its range and—the more that people have thought about him—in its meanings. If the pivotal themes of America are success and failure, Grant's was an exemplary American life.

A study in the mysteries of the ordinary, he went from poverty to presidency and back to poverty again—from obscurity and shame before the Civil War, to all that the country had to offer in the way of power and glory, and then back to ruin once more.

There was a familiar American residue of the biblical in the story (Matthew 20:16: "The last shall be first"... and, as it turned out here, the last again). For a hundred years, Grant was ranked among the worst of presidents (down there with Buchanan and Harding). But the verdict has been reversed on appeal. Despite the sullying alcoholism, the terrible butcher's bills, and the Gilded Age corruption, he has begun to achieve historical radiance.

Grant seemed to encompass the country's binaries (again, that word), the doubleness: Enlightenment ideals compromised by violent squalors. And yet he emerged, by grace and the mystery of his character, on the right side of things after all. His contradictory life touched the country's major themes; above all, it became a case study in the decisive American alternatives (success and failure), a theme that reverberates in the new Gilded Age of the 21st century. Success and failure in the American mind are remnants of the Calvinist's binaries of salvation and damnation.

He became, among other things, an inquiry into the great American problem: how to reconcile virtue and power. He and Lincoln struggled endlessly with that.

Grant was a relatively slight figure (5'8" and sometimes as light as 135 lbs.), a seemingly unprepossessing and even shabby man. He hit hard times after he was forced out of the army for drunkenness and made a mess of farming at the spread he called Hardscrabble. He sold his gold watch and chain to buy Christmas presents for his children. These are old stories, the Grant myth, the American extremes.

Then came Fort Sumter and his astonishing transformation—a classic American resurrection. George McClellan was a master of military preparation: the army as glorious *tableau vivant*. Other generals (the dithering Rosecrans in Tennessee, Meade in his failure to pursue Lee after Gettysburg) also had "the slows." But Grant's practice of war was ruthlessly and single-mindedly active—daring on occasion, but relentless, American: as brutal as necessary in battle and most gentle and generous when it was over. His genius consisted in his ability to absorb quantities of information, not only as to the numbers of an opposing army and its fortifications and artillery but also as to landscape, weather, the morale of his men and the enemy's men, the will and talents of his officers and the enemy's, the state of the army's health and rations, and when it had last eaten. He had the Napoleonic instinct—a way of knowing how everything would be at 3 o'clock tomorrow afternoon. He was willing to act and take chances and fight. Action creates fresh reality. It was the great secret: A battlefield in motion is the river of Heraclitus, changing from one instant to the next. He had the character to enter entirely into the tragedy of war, which he hated; he was willing "to face the arithmetic," Lincoln said.

He rose to glory, the first genius of industrial warfare, commander of the million-man army that ended slavery and saved the United States. Lincoln and Grant presided over the regeneration of the American story. It was a nice touch that Grant looked only slightly better than a bum when he accepted Lee's surrender at Appomattox. Lee showed up as if dressed for a costume ball. The terms of surrender were generous: Keep the sidearms and horses for the spring plowing.

But Appomattox was merely the end of one phase of an American drama that goes on and on.

In the upheavals of 2020, Black Lives Matter protestors attacked statues of Ulysses Grant, of all people—presumably for the primitive reason that he was a powerful white man.

As president, Grant did his best with Reconstruction; he suppressed the Ku Klux Klan, encouraged freedmen's rights, and promoted their full citizenship. As a champion of black rights, Grant was much admired by Frederick Douglass and others, and bitterly denounced by whites who organized the Jim Crow resistance that restored so much of the totalitarian status quo ante. After 150 years, the country is still sorting out the interrupted business of Reconstruction and the terms and conditions applying to the citizenship of black people. We live among the aftershocks.

In the 21st century, people do not quite dismiss possibilities that would have seemed absurd a year or two ago. Former Indian prime minister Jawarhalal Nehru said that "the Americans are the most hysterical people in the world, with the possible exception of the Bengalis."

If the South cherished myths of heroic aristocracy, Grant represented a sort of Roundhead austerity, Methodist in tone, an American plain-style that came to its finest expression just at the end of his life, when—broke again (because he and his son Buck got taken in and bankrupted by a Bernie Madoff–style Wall Street Ponzi artist named Ferdinand Ward)—he set out to write his memoirs in order to raise cash to support his family after he was gone.

Grant was dying of cancer of the mouth and throat (you cannot smoke twenty cigars a day without consequence). Over the course of a year, with publishing arrangements handled by his friend Mark Twain, Grant (in pain relieved occasionally by morphine) produced his *Personal*

Memoirs of Ulysses S. Grant, one of the two or three greatest military memoirs in history.

Listen to Grant's prose, the work of a dying soldier writing two thousand years after Caesar's *Commentaries on the Gallic War*, even longer than that after Xenophon's *Anabasis*, and fourteen years before the birth of Ernest Hemingway:

> We were now to operate in a different country from any we had before seen in Virginia. The roads were wide and good, and the country well cultivated.... Engineers and staff officers were put to the dangerous duty of supplying the place of both maps and guides.... Our course was south, and we took all roads leading in that direction which would not separate the army too widely.

Grant had about him a mysterious stateliness. He began his *Memoirs* with this flawless line: "My family is American, and has been for generations, in all its branches, direct and collateral."

Grant's recent biographers (Ron Chernow and Jean Edward Smith, for example) have refuted two long-embedded judgments: the first being that Grant's wartime success was the result not of his military greatness but of Northern superiority in industrial capacity and in sheer manpower (cannon fodder at the service of a general in chief whom Mary Todd Lincoln called a "butcher"). The next was that his two terms as president justified the verdict (encouraged by the Southern school of historians) that Grant presided over a corrupt and otherwise undistinguished administration that made him one of the three worst presidents in American history.

Chernow's biography, *Grant*, reminded 21st-century readers of the distinction between character and personality.

Grant belonged to an American Culture of Character that shaped its ideas of moral education around the study of Plutarch and Cicero, and the writings of Benjamin Franklin and the example of George Washington, and that focused upon such virtues as integrity, humility, honesty, courage, fidelity, justice, patience, industry, modesty, and adherence to the Golden Rule.

But in the 1920s, after the Great War, the American Culture of Personality began to take over from the Culture of Character. Modern advertising, public relations, and salesmanship perfected themselves, attended by a postwar secularism, disillusion, and cynicism about the traditional virtues of courage, honor, and fortitude, and all of that: the *Dulce et decorum est pro patria mori* that came to seem grotesque after Ypres and the Somme. Popular religion adopted the techniques of modern advertising, public relations, and mass psychology—the arts of crowd manipulation—and produced Aimee Semple McPherson. Sinclair Lewis's *Elmer Gantry* became the model of Evangelical salesmanship.

Grant lives on, in wistful memory, as a hero of the lost Culture of American character. Even his famous flaw, his drinking, was not in the end a flaw, but instead the struggle that allowed him to go on trying to perfect his character.

♪

After the Civil War came the stupendous American fortunes, the Gilded Age, the malefactors of great wealth and privilege, and, eventually, in the case of the Baptist Rockefellers, say, the benefactions whereby the children and grandchildren of some founding pirates gave back the wealth a hundredfold.

American exceptionalism becomes confused when huge misfortunes come: Such catastrophes (economic depressions and other afflictions, including the pandemic of 2020) seem to be a betrayal of the country's official understanding of itself and its raison d'être, the gentleman's agreement that named Americans as God's chosen.

11

Atlanta newspapers printed stories about four alleged rapes of white women by black men. The rumors precipitated race riots that went on for five days in September of 1906.

"Large crowds of white men and boys filled the streets that afternoon and into the evening [of September 22]," according to an account by the historian Raymond W. Smock.

> The crowd became a mob that marched down Decatur Street and other black sections of the city, destroying black businesses, pulling blacks from streetcars and beating them, and shooting and killing two dozen or more citizens before the riot ended. Five whites also died in the rioting, including two policemen and a woman who suffered a heart attack when she saw the mob.

The state militia was mobilized but failed to stop the violence. Some blacks took up guns to defend their property. Others fled, looking for safety in the countryside. Walter White, who was thirteen at the time and would one day become president of the NAACP, remembered that his father handed him a gun and told him to shoot any of the mob who came onto their property. White said that it was on that night that he realized he was black.

❧

White was black, and what was Booker T. Washington? He was the preeminent black American leader and spokesman at that time—a slave at birth who would dine at the White House with Theodore Roosevelt. He founded Tuskegee Institute in Alabama, and, in 1895, delivered the famous speech that formulated the Atlanta Compromise. Some thought—some still think—that he accommodated himself too thoroughly to white power in America, that he functioned as a sort of honorary white man himself and that he had become an Uncle Tom and that his very success represented a betrayal of his own black people.

In a speech given at the Cotton States and International Exposition, Washington proposed what would come to be called the "Atlanta Compromise," a bargain with the white South, promising in effect that Negroes would submit to white political rule; would not seek to secure civil rights (the vote, equal access to public accommodations); and would tolerate segregation and discrimination and not retaliate against racist behavior. In exchange, Washington suggested, blacks should be unmolested as they sought to improve themselves with vocational or industrial education, learning basic skills and trades, and going about their business in an unobtrusive and unthreatening fashion. His idea was a great hit when he proposed it in 1895; it made him famous and was praised as the way forward, as the work of the country's racial stateman, decent and intelligent and (to whites) reassuringly deferential. Even the mandarin W. E. B. Du Bois, advocate of the Talented Tenth, praised the speech at the time. But later on, Du Bois decided it would not do; he coined the phrase "Atlanta compromise"—the word "compromise" here indicating a defeat—in order to denigrate it. He even suggested that it was that speech that led on to the Atlanta riots of 1906.

The riots deeply disconcerted Booker Washington. He was forty-nine years old, the most famous black man in America: a friend and confidant of such white millionaires and philanthropists as Andrew Carnegie. He was said to be the man who had gone further to solve the American race question than anyone else.

Born into slavery in Virginia just before the Civil War and raised in poverty, sleeping on a pile of rags on a dirt floor, feeding on scraps, and put to work as a small boy in the salt furnaces and coal mines of West Virginia, Booker Taliaferro (pronounced "Tolliver") Washington represented (as did Frederick Douglass, only more so) a Negro version of the rags-to-riches stories that were popular in the Gilded Age. Carnegie himself had been a fine example—a poor Scotch immigrant boy whom the American magic transformed into the titan of US Steel. Horatio Alger's dime novels told the story over and over of the poor but clean-living, plucky lad who succeeded by dint of fair play and luck, and by giving himself over to—by actually *becoming*—the American Dream.

Booker Washington passed through many dangers, toils, and snares, as the hymn said, to reach Hampton Institute when he was a sixteen-year-old boy. Hampton was an academy run by Samuel Armstrong, the handsome son of Sandwich Island missionaries. He had been the youngest general in the Civil War and went on to start the institute in order to educate Negroes to become teachers who would raise the race and save it.

The exemplary young Booker T. Washington (gray-eyed, light-skinned, relentlessly positive, shrewd, and unstoppable) took Armstrong as his model and ideal. He started Tuskegee Institute from scratch in Macon County, east of Montgomery, Alabama. He took in young black people from the countryside, requiring each to bring a toothbrush and to use it; he developed an ideology of the toothbrush, believing that dental hygiene was the key, the start of a successful life. A toothbrush was the beginning of personal order and self-respect.

When Washington first arrived at Tuskegee, there were no buildings, there was no school. There was only the idea of a school and the state's authorization for it. He and the students built everything, using, among other things, bricks fired in their own kiln, which they built and then taught themselves to use. He would boast in his memoir *Up from Slavery* that the bricks they made at Tuskegee Institute became the finest in Alabama and that white builders would seek them out and pay top dollar for them.

Washington was a man of extraordinary gifts and complexity, a hero and a great dissembler. His mind was clear and direct and yet Machiavellian. He was a smiling public man and also a guerrilla and secret agent operating behind enemy lines. He appeased the totalitarian white South, keeping to the lines of the Atlanta Compromise, never threatening, always dignified and subtly deferential, speaking in high-minded and eloquent generalities (he was an excellent public speaker) about advancing both races—everyone happy together. At the same time, he built an extraordinary network of friendships and contacts with white Northern men of money, whom he impressed and induced to contribute handsomely to Tuskegee.

Tuskegee Institute flourished as a model of what he called industrial education—the task being to teach young Negroes the methods of farming and mechanics, carpentry, and other useful trades and arts. Washington was suspicious of intellectuals and Big Ideas.

His idea was simple enough, and big enough, and brilliant and, more than one hundred years later, it still has (despite everything) immense appeal.

⋟

In 1953, the political philosopher and historian of ideas Isaiah Berlin published an essay—soon to be famous in a minor way—called "The Hedgehog and the Fox." His point of departure was an enigmatic fragment by the ancient Greek poet Archilochus: "The fox knows many things, the hedgehog knows one big thing." Berlin used the distinction to discuss Dostoevsky and Tolstoy, but soon, in certain sets, there was a new game of categories in which the players assigned people to one or the other of the binaries. Franklin Roosevelt, everyone agreed, was a fox.

Booker Washington was both animals at once.

As a fox, he knew many, many things, and he was elaborate and subtle and secretive in the ways he manipulated that knowledge. He hired spies to keep track of his enemies and played unscrupulous tricks upon them—as when, for example, he arranged to have a newspaper reporter attend a perfectly blameless interracial dinner and report that his black adversaries had behaved lewdly with white socialites in low-cut gowns.

But the hedgehog in Booker Washington knew this one big thing: that money is the language and the common denominator in America. If blacks were to succeed, they must learn to make money, and to keep it, over the long haul.

He undertook systematically to bring money to American blacks, the children and grandchildren of slaves. He undertook to build a solid and impregnable black middle class, operating on the premise that American blacks would become full Americans to the extent that they had money.

His critics—rhetoricians and moral leaders, eloquent and sometimes fiery writers—had their minds fixed on black Americans' *rights*, and beyond that, on their dignity. Washington—even at the cost of some momentary loss of dignity and self-esteem—sought to build them the fundamental thing they lacked: an economic *role* in the society. He calculated that rights and respect would follow the money.

There is a functional difference between a legal right and a material role. Washington saw that, in the American scheme of things, the material role had a better chance of ensuring the legal right than the other way around. He had the thoroughly American intuition that money would make all things whole and possible for blacks—that, over years and decades, money would carry them into full citizenship in the mainstream of American life.

He laid out a program for blacks, especially Southern blacks, in which they might use the quintessential American instrument and language of money (acquired through trades and business; learned, as such things had to be learned, conscientiously and in detail, from the bottom up—the Benjamin Franklin way) in order to lift up the entire African American people and give them a basic equality measured in dollars, which was the American way of judging things. From this equality, other forms of dignity and respect and political power would naturally flow. Racism tends to vanish—to flee, or at least to go into hiding—in the face of real money. Money commands respect as a rule. And if the respect doesn't come, who cares? You have the money.

Washington knew that mere rhetoric and mere politics—symbolism, unsupported by dollars that have been earned by blacks themselves—would not do the job. For blacks, the way to power in American society, as he understood it, was for them to buy their way in—to take the organic approach, to grow a black American economy in the same way that a farmer raises crops. Start with the seeds.

W. E. B. Du Bois, or William Edward Burghardt Du Bois (who pronounced his name "dew BOICE," rhyming with voice) was born and raised in Great Barrington, Massachusetts, and went to school mostly with white children. He was not made to feel especially different from the others. He would study at the University of Berlin and become the first black to receive a doctorate at Harvard University.

Du Bois was an intellectual and something of a dandy, who wore spats and carried a cane; he became a Marxist and eventually fled America to spend his last years in Ghana. When he first went to the South to conduct a scholarly study of Negro life, he traveled as a tourist—something of a naïf. Booker Washington was a native son. He did not have to ask questions or take notes.

Washington contemplated the Atlanta riots with dismay. As his biographer Raymond W. Smock observed:

> Washington saw race violence in class terms. The better classes of white people did not engage in lynching, and the better classes of black people were not criminals. Blacks "who owned homes, who are taxpayers, who have a trade or other regular occupation," and those with an education were not likely to commit crimes. Washington was trying to make a reasoned appeal to tone down Atlanta's incendiary atmosphere, but some of his remarks could easily be construed to justify violence. He did not stop after noting the better class of blacks who did not commit crime; he also felt the need to talk about those who did.

Washington's maneuvers of deference and conciliation sometimes raised questions about where his loyalty lay.

"Which is the class that is guilty, as a rule, of criminal action?" he asked before answering his own question: "They are the loafers, the drunkards and gamblers, men for the main part without permanent employment, who own no homes, who have no bank account, who glide from one community to another without interest in any one spot." What Washington could never control was how the newspapers played his remarks. The *Atlanta Constitution* gave a fair account of the speech but gave the story an incendiary headline: "LAW-BREAKING NEGROES WORST MENACE TO RACE."

Washington preached nonviolence. Du Bois, on the other hand, rushed home to Atlanta when the riots erupted and sat with a loaded shotgun in his lap, ready to repel the white mob.

On the train back to Atlanta from Alabama, Du Bois composed a poem called "The Litany at Atlanta":

> Bewildered we are, and passion-tost, mad with the madness of a
> mobbed and mocked and murdered people; straining at the armposts
> of Thy Throne, we raise our shackled hands and charge Thee, God,
> by the bones of our stolen fathers, by the tears of our dead mothers,
> by the very blood of Thy crucified Christ: *What meaneth this?* Tell us
> the Plan; give us the *Sign!*
>> *Keep not thou silence, O God!*

After the Atlanta riots of 1906, Ray Stannard Baker, writing in *McClure's* and the *American Magazine*, undertook a massive study of American race relations; in 1908, it was published as a book: *Following the Color Line.*

He noted that now there were "Two Great Negro Parties" in America, one headed by Booker T. Washington and the other by W. E. B. Du Bois. Baker wrote: "Nothing has been more remarkable in the recent history of the Negro than Washington's rise to influence as a leader, and the spread of his ideals of education and progress." He continued, "The party led by Washington is made up of the masses of the common people; the radical party [that of Du Bois and his Niagara Movement], on the other hand, represents what may be called the intellectuals." Washington represented the South; Du Bois the North.

African blacks packed onboard slave ships off the coast of Sierra Leone were reduced, by force—demoted, degraded—to the status of property in the hands of property owners.

Booker T. Washington invented a strategy to reverse the process, with the goal of transforming American blacks from property to property owners, from commodity back to humanity.

He succeeded and he failed. Du Bois seemed to have won the argument. Washington would be dismissed as an Uncle Tom. In his novel *Invisible Man*, Ralph Ellison, a graduate of Tuskegee, turned him into a sinister and scheming hypocrite, a Svengali of the "Tuskegee machine."

Booker Washington's program, if it had been more determinedly followed than it was, might have resulted in more black material success and in less white racist sentiment in regard to blacks. Who knows? Washington believed that the only way truly to improve the lives of black Americans was through the slow, steady building of a black American economy, skills, trades, and professions: black banks, black factories, black corporations, black ownership, black leadership in communities. *Black money.*

But in the quickening pace and rapidly unfolding changes of the 20th century (automobiles, radio, migrations into cities, transformations), it was W. E. B. Du Bois who seemed to carry the argument. The experience of 1919—when terrible urban race riots broke out in the summer after the armistice—was crucial. The Klan came back to life and was in full cry in the years that followed. It even conducted a massive march on Washington in 1926. In that atmosphere, Booker Washington's message of (sly, manipulative) deference to whites and slow, (only apparently) submissive apprenticeship to the white economy seemed craven—seemed mere appeasement, seemed humiliating. The reaction was understandable, but Washington made the better case, I have sometimes thought, and perhaps he still does. But, on the other hand, I have no idea.

Which of them was right—Du Bois or Washington? Again, the American binaries—and American what-ifs. The Black Lives Matter eruptions of 2020 would radically alter the terms of the old Du Bois-Washington discussion and would even make that discussion seem to be irrelevant—out of date. But when the moment has passed, I suspect the two opposing models will remain pertinent.

Again, we are talking about the emotions of American money. Du Bois and Washington represent different calculations as to pride, defiance or deference, and self-suppression. There was a psychic price to be paid if an American black followed Booker Washington's way, and who was to say at what moment that price became too steep?

12

They buried George Floyd yesterday in Houston. Joe Biden was there. Al Sharpton spoke. Everyone wore masks, which lent to the occasion an air of Dada.

It was a working of haphazard metaphysics that all of this turmoil was started by a scrap of money or pseudomoney—the $20 bill that George Floyd used to pay for cigarettes at a Minneapolis convenience story. The clerk decided the bill was counterfeit...and called the police...and the police arrested Floyd...and put him in handcuffs...and killed him...

And the country exploded.

Money and tobacco—items drifting in Brownian motion through history from Jefferson's Virginia to Minneapolis. These things are accidental...but still.

The wind shear that I spoke of in the country has, if anything, grown stronger and more dramatic, and harder to understand. The stock market has come booming back, somewhat weirdly. The Dow closed yesterday at 27,272—back to where it was before. There is great hope, it seems, for the reopening of things, for the revival of an economy that had been suddenly put into an emergency Cinderella's sleep by the pandemic.

Yet race demonstrations continue everywhere. Outrage at the videotaped death of George Floyd has fused with the political campaign against Donald Trump's reelection. November is five months away, but everywhere on the left there is anxiety that the election will be canceled and a state of emergency declared.

Progressives say that Trump will stage a coup d'état. The Left demands the "defunding" of the police, which means either reducing police department budgets and giving the money to social programs for blacks or else eliminating police departments altogether.

Conservatives claim that America is in the midst of a coup d'état conducted by a radical left using the death of George Floyd to exploit black grievances and to manipulate whites' indignant sympathy in order, in the midst of pandemic, to seize power and overthrow the norms of an American society that they consider to be fascist, racist, and so on. Conservative friends speak of the Left now as "the American Taliban."

Frustrated by the lockdown and the riots, people are moving out of the city. We meet them walking on our remote dirt road. In the last two or three months, every house that was available up here for sale or rental has been taken. The migrations give some inkling that poor New York City is in a state of decomposition.

There was a full moon the other night. The coyotes have been abnormally active and noisy. Yesterday we saw the big one—the alpha male who leaves his scat conspicuously on our paths as a greeting—walking in plain sight, carelessly, among the apple trees beside the house. This is unusual coyote behavior; normally they prefer to stay out of sight, although they don't mind howling and yipping when the moon is full or their blood is up.

The coyotes are having a luxurious season, eating well. Rabbits are abundant. So are fawns. But the coyotes mill so close around the house that I worry about our dog Teddy. I went out at dusk among the apple trees and fired off the shotgun a couple of times into the air—to warn the coyotes to back off a little. To observe social distancing.

It is a sweet early June, but there is something jittery and disturbed in the air—the new people, the strange sight of everyone wearing masks, the few restaurants in town closed up or else offering curbside pickup of dinners that a masked waiter brings out just at dusk and, reaching gingerly through the window, places on the passenger seat, the smells of the cooked food (meatloaf, salmon, garlic, the smells all mingled) gusting out of the paper bags.

Something odd: Two days ago, when we got up in the morning, we found the kitchen door wide open. We normally lock it at night and do so especially these days when so many strangers have come up from the city. But there was the door, wide open. We were certain we had locked it. We found nothing missing or disturbed in the house.

But now I sleep with the shotgun standing in a corner—loaded, with the safety on.

13

In the summer of 1893, a professor of English at Wellesley, Katharine Lee Bates, traveled west by train from Boston, stopping in Chicago to visit the World's Columbian Exposition—the "White City." Then she rode south and west, through Kansas wheat fields, toward the Rockies, and came at last to Colorado Springs, where she spent the summer. Looking out at the country from Pikes Peak, she had a vision.

She wrote a poem that eventually became *America the Beautiful*. The White City became "Thine alabaster cities gleam, undimmed by human tears!" Kansas supplied "spacious skies" and "amber waves of grain." The Rockies became the "purple mountain majesties." Her poem was set to music a few years later and became a sort of alternative national anthem.

Bates captured the country's vaguely religious patriotism—the sentimental and radiant self-reverence: *God shed his grace on thee*. Funny that she composed her rhapsody at a graceless, bitter moment of the country's history. America's manifest destiny was not manifest just then.

The 1890s began with the US Army's massacre of several hundred Lakota Sioux at Wounded Knee. The buffalo of the Great Plains were nearly extinct. The historian Frederick Jackson Turner announced the end of the American frontier. The year that Katharine Bates wrote her poem, a financial panic precipitated the worst economic depression that had happened, until then, in the country's history.

In the 1890s, labor-management battles at Andrew Carnegie's Homestead steel plant in Pennsylvania left eighteen people dead. Coxey's Army of the unemployed descended on Washington. In a nationwide Pullman strike, thirty-four railway union members were gunned down.

Eugene V. Debs, arrested for his role in the strike, spent six months in an Illinois prison reading Karl Marx. He would go on to run for president five times as the candidate of the Socialist Party of America.

In Chicago, the World's Columbian Exposition was set afire and seven buildings in the alabaster city burned to the ground. Jim Crow ruled in the South. More than 1,100 blacks were lynched. The Supreme Court affirmed *Plessy v. Ferguson* ("Separate but equal"), which became the law of the land for the next fifty-eight years.

The two versions of the United States—the heroic ideal and the raw reality—fought like Jacob and Esau in the womb. Each appraisal of the country—"a City on a Hill" and "the last best hope of earth" vs. the monster of jingo, greed, and genocide—had its elements of truth, but, at the same time, bore witness to an American tendency toward exaggeration, especially in its spasms of self-esteem and self-abasement. Americans have been sometimes naïvely spooked—especially since the 1960s—by the distance between what the country ought to be and what it is. A remnant Calvinism has deviled the civic conscience. If the country or the individual was not perfect, then it must be damned.

Still, the American *Ought* did good work in encouraging the American *Is* to improve itself. Each narrative and each catastrophe has warned the country not to be too sure of itself.

In its troubled self-assessment, America would become a split screen of the great and the ignoble. The bet was that, over time, the net good would outweigh the net bad, and that the country would evolve, with ups and downs, toward something better. Americans have sometimes been good at evolving—sometimes not. The country has proceeded on a premise of hope—on expectation, an assumed tendency toward perfection, or at least toward expansion and inclusion: Slaves got emancipated and women attained the right to vote and immigrants assimilated and thrived over the generations. Time is an inclined plane, the path of progress and improvement and something better.

Is it still true? Was it ever true? Some, in the year 2020, in the time of pandemic, have become ambitious about abolishing the idea of mere progress in favor of revolutionary change.

America the Beautiful emerged as an unofficial anthem only after the depression of the 1890s was over and America had become newly self-confident. Americans adopted an imperialist swagger after the Spanish-American War and the advent of Teddy Roosevelt, whose idea of fun was rough and tumble, either boyish or slightly insane: fox hunting with a broken arm, as he did once, or finishing his speech during the 1912 Bull Moose campaign after someone had just shot him in the chest. After a parade of relatively colorless presidents (Rutherford B. Hayes, Chester A. Arthur, James A. Garfield, Grover Cleveland, William McKinley), Roosevelt reaffirmed for Americans the importance of character—which, in him, was garishly embellished by personality—in shaping the country's history.

14

How was American money to organize itself for good?

Two schools of thought took shape.

The first of them sought the moral redemption of American wealth by philanthropy.

The second model sought to achieve that goal by means of government.

The philanthropic model amounted, in effect, to Christianity's reply to Charles Darwin. In the raw Darwinian dramas of capitalism, John D. Rockefeller would accumulate money—sinful dollars in the millions. Ida Tarbell and other voices of progressive American Virtue would assail the Malefactors of Great Wealth, just as Jesus assailed the money-changers in the temple.

But, if all went well in the American scheme, the fortune would in time be purified and returned to the people, in Christian love—for John D. was a pious Baptist—in the form of hospitals and universities and museums and libraries. John D. Rockefeller the Son, "Mr. Junior," as the family staff called him—a man as different from his father as Jesus Christ was from the God of the Old Testament—would preside over an astonishing public benevolence. He would accomplish the redemption—of his father, of the family, of capitalist America itself—through Good Works that would hint, in this world, at the Kingdom of God to come.

Meantime, guided by the publicist Ivy Lee, old man Rockefeller, villain and plutocrat in the Ida Tarbell version, would undergo a moral transformation and become a twinkling, grandfatherly eccentric handing out dimes and maxims on frugality.

The moral journey of money from sin to virtue would recapitulate the immigrant story—a passage across the waters from the sinful world of the old dispensation to the redemption of the new.

Then came the second school of thought. In the emergency of the Great Depression that followed the Great Crash, Franklin Roosevelt, Harry Hopkins, and the rest attempted to rationalize the national benevolence, in most humane essentials, through government bureaucracy. The Lord giveth and the Lord taketh away was the idea. The IRS takes money away and bureaucracy returns it, in various forms of public good. The workings of justice in such distributions are imperfect and sometimes corrupt, big government's duties being more diverse and comprehensive than those of philanthropy.

Those were the crude, basic models of the story that, in turn, would organize the country's politics.

15

Years ago, I persuaded the editors at *TIME* magazine, where I worked as an essayist writing on politics and other things, to send me and my friend Neil Leifer, the great photographer, to Kenya to do a long essay about the animals of Africa. I lived for a time with Masai tribesmen in the Loita Hills in dun-colored, sparsely wooded country, a few hours' drive southwest of Nairobi.

I walked each morning to the river with Moses and his cattle. Moses was the elder chief among his people—a handsome, charismatic man of about thirty. He spoke English, and because he had worked from time to time with visiting European and American scientists and ethnographers, he had skills and possessions that were otherwise alien to the Masai—a powerful Maglite, for example, that he wielded like a Jedi lightsaber when (contrary to the usual Masai practice) he ventured out from the *boma* into the blackness of the African night. He directed the Maglite's beam here and there in the tremendous dark and picked out the shining eyes of hyenas, wild dogs, and other animals that hunted at night.

The cattle were Moses's money, his great wealth. I suppose there were more than one hundred, but when I asked him the number, he became evasive. To ask this question was a faux pas. Masai do not like to be specific about their cows—a reticence that you can also find in a Henry James novel, in which the source of a family's money is not mentioned in polite company.

Moses knew each of his beasts by name. They were high-humped Boran cattle, of ancient design, and might have been the same ones plodding through the fields of the Pharaohs. (An eon ago, drought had driven the pastoralists of Egypt far south in search of pasture, and that accounted for the presence of their descendants in the Loita Hills.)

Moses explained to me that his cattle observed a set order of march when proceeding to the river: The same white one would lead the procession, and the next one was always the same, and the next, and the next; and the same cow (also mostly white, as I recall) always brought up the rear.

One morning as we went along through the forest, the cattle—all of them at the same instant—smelled lion. Abruptly, they all raised their heads with their great horns and bawled and bawled. Moses whisper shouted to me, "Lion!" and with his spear and *rungu* (a bulbous hardwood knobkerrie that he could throw with impressive accuracy and effect) and *simi* (the Masai's last line of defense, a sort of short sword or machete), rushed toward the source of the smell.

But the lion ran away. It slipped off among the thorn trees and the lion-colored grasses. Moses strolled back to me and we took up our discussion where we had left off.

The lion had intended a daring daylight bank robbery, but it aborted. Moses continued herding his assets to the river, where they would luxuriously and lazily drink, and he and I would sit in the thin shade of an acacia tree.

The Masai made regular withdrawals from their cow-money in the form of blood and milk. They would deftly open a vein in the beast's neck and extrude sufficient blood to pinken their milk and spike it with protein, and then they would cover the wound with mud—an operation to which the animal submitted as impassively as an ATM.

The Masai would also eat doughy meal-cakes that they would brown like biscuits on the fire. Everything in the intimate Masai world has a dense but not unpleasing smell of wood smoke.

Only now and then, on special occasions, did the Masai dip into their capital by actually slaughtering one of their beasts. I witnessed one such event when a wildlife expert named Jonah Western took me to an *orpul*—a Masai warrior's coming-of-age ceremony: a preparation for the lion hunt that was a required test of manhood.

We flew in Jonah's single-engine aircraft across the Laikipia plain. We landed in a flat, stony clearing and a half-dozen young warriors interrupted their feasting to come out of the forest to greet us and stroke the plane with sensual admiration. Jonah took their picture with a Polaroid camera and as the photograph developed, they clustered around him to see their images coalescing and emerging slowly out of white fog on the sticky rectangle. As they grasped the magic they were seeing, they leaped and laughed in wonder.

As part of the Masai's customarily elaborate decoration, several of them wore black plastic-strapped digital watches whose batteries had long since expired. No matter to them. The Masai are a beautiful people, and often vain, much given to self-decoration—with bracelets and swags of of bright beads in primary colors. Once, up in the Matthews Range of Northern Kenya, we were traveling by foot with the party of Masai who managed our donkeys. One of us had a shaving mirror that got broken. Next day, one of the Masai appeared with a new headdress. He had taken a piece of the broken mirror—a fragment shaped like a rhombus—and, using leather thongs, had fastened it in the middle of his forehead: a striking and handsome effect.

At an *orpul*, young warriors withdraw into the forest and kill one of their cattle, and then, over the course of several days, proceed to consume it—all of it except the hooves, horns, and bones. They keep a cook fire going and methodically cut up and grill or boil the animal and ingest it—the steaks, the organs, the entrails, the marrow, and the brain. The feast gives their systems an unaccustomed shock of protein that causes their eyes and their very skin to glisten, and their bodies to vibrate with excitement and (the point of it all) with courage to face the lion.

It is money well spent from the point of view of the Masai's sociobiology—an investment in the future, a ceremonial part of turning a boy into a man: not just a man but a warrior.

Moses and the warriors and herdboys of the Masai walk their unwieldy assets around the Loita Hills. They give their wealth an airing and a drink at the river, and then they lock them up again in the safety of the *boma*, a kraal of mud huts enclosed by a high fence made of stacked thorn branches to keep out the lions and leopards at night. The lion has a fondness for beef.

A people's money may express their character. It may become their way of life. In that sense, money connects the ways the Masai to the novels of Jane Austen.

16

Donald Trump, an American original, has understood money's subtle modulations of unreality, its talent as mythmaker. He is a phenomenon of self-invention—like Fitzgerald's Jay Gatsby, who started out with nothing, as nothing—Jay Gatz—in rural North Dakota.

Or like Bob Dylan, another self-invented American character. He borrowed an essential persona from Woody Guthrie and went from there. What did he prove? In America, a great deal can come from nothing at all, or next to nothing. The most distinguished blossoming of that idea can be seen in Abraham Lincoln.

Robert Zimmerman was born in May of 1941 and emerged from the town of Hibbing, in the same Minnesota that gave to American literature Sinclair Lewis's hometown of Sauk Centre, which he called Gopher Prairie in *Main Street*. Hibbing, Minnesota, lies in the Iron Range, which by the time of Bob Zimmerman's adolescence in the 1950s was strip-mined, disfigured, exhausted, and all but defunct.

In 2005, Martin Scorsese made a documentary about Dylan called *No Direction Home*. It emphasized the dreariness of Hibbing, the ordinariness: Scorsese gave the place an atmosphere that was bleak, sinister, heartbreaking, stifling. All politics begins in storylines.

If Hibbing had been filmed through a friendlier, more sentimental lens—the optic of Thornton Wilder or Norman Rockwell or Frank Capra—it might be thought to have been a sweet, touching, even profoundly meaningful place. If Scorsese had set out to make a documentary about the heartbreak of the hollowed-out American working class and middle class abandoned by globalization and left to decay in so many parts of the formerly flourishing industrial Midwest, then Hibbing would have seemed poignant, sympathetic.

The damning scenes in Scorsese's version include shots of a small-town parade on Main Street. The veterans marching in uniform, in a scene in which Scorsese manages to convey the idea of oppressive, Know Nothing militarism, now become merely seedy and depressing. The scene lingers in the mind as an act of casual defamation. Scorsese casts the old men in uniform—and the town itself—as failures. To be a failure in America is to be that most to-be-feared-and-despised of American things—a sort of leper.

But many of the men were veterans of World War II. It is possible that some of them had been with units that liberated Hitler's concentration camps. They would have landed at Normandy, perhaps fought their way across France, and crossed the Rhine. They might have fought in the Battle of the Bulge or in the Hürtgen Forest. It was terrible duty, fatal to many thousands of their friends and fellow GIs. And many of them, surviving the war, would have been happy to make it back, alive, to Hibbing, where they received and deserved a hero's welcome.

In Scorsese's film, the men who crushed Hitler's militarism were subtly arraigned as representing a sort of Hitleristic American militarism themselves. Scorsese's portrait of Dylan's hometown emphasizes the smallness of the town, the bleakness—the spiritual emptiness, the conformity. Generational politics may be vicious, oblivious, ungrateful. The effect is something of the same debunking in which Sinclair Lewis indulged when he wrote *Babbitt* and *Main Street*. As I have said, we all come from different planets; the difference (in how one sees America, for example) is often moral.

Hibbing is where Andrew B. "Bus Andy" Anderson and Carl Eric Wickman pooled their resources in 1914 and bought a Hupmobile, the vehicle with which they started the Greyhound bus company. Was that a great American story of heartland entrepreneurship, the creation of an iconic American brand? Or did it speak of stupidity, banality?

These waves of denigration and mockery are heartbreaking—they mark acts of abandonment and repudiation: gestures of parricide.

On the other hand, success is success, and if you become famous, you can probably always go home again. If you do not become a success, you may still go home, but no one will notice, or perhaps if they do, they will write you off as white trash, as a deplorable, a redneck, a racist, something in that line of villains.

But it's different if you become famous. So it is that a website boosting Hibbing's attractions ("Strip mining is represented by the original steam shovel stripping away the worthless bits of earth to reveal the ore") includes these items:

> Bob Dylan Sculpture: During the... Mines & Pines Festival an unveiling of the life-size papier-mâché sculpture of Bob Dylan took place. The sculpture, created by Ann Schnortz, is now on display in the Hibbing Public Library.

> Bob Dylan Display: The exhibit was started in 1991 but has grown throughout the years. Many items have been purchased or donated by interested persons and are included in the display. The exhibit was redesigned and updated in 2003 to include the more recent work of Bob Dylan.

And so it was that Dylan came to be memorialized in his hometown. In a similar fashion, Sauk Centre learned, eventually, to be proud of Sinclair Lewis, who had defamed the place and satirized its provincialism; and Asheville, North Carolina, managed to declare itself proud of Thomas Wolfe, who portrayed the town grimly enough in his novel *You Can't Go Home Again,* published in 1940.

America was started by people repudiating their origins in Europe and recreating themselves elsewhere, in America. The pattern would become habitual. Lewis wrote *Main Street* as a brilliant act of repudiation, although the novel is a subtler and more interesting critique of the American small town than its more simpleminded admirers understood. When the Swedish Academy voted to bestow the Nobel Prize upon Lewis in 1930, they made it clear that he had won it because of *Babbitt* and its attack on American bourgeois values. On hearing of the prize, Calvin Coolidge remarked: "No necessity exists for becoming excited."

The poet Edgar Lee Masters's *Spoon River Anthology* amounted to a similar, sometimes savage repudiation of origins. So did Sherwood Anderson's *Winesburg, Ohio*. The portrayal of small American towns as hypocritical, mean spirited, and stultifying is a commonplace of American literature. H. L. Mencken had a polemical, burlesquing kind of genius for damning the small town—Dayton, Tennessee, for example, the site of the Scopes Trial in 1925.

Bobby Zimmerman, plagiarizing the manner and accent and persona of Woody Guthrie—troubadour of the boxcars and the Dust Bowl—invented Bob Dylan and became an immense American success. He wound up with a Nobel Prize, as did Sinclair Lewis and Ernest Hemingway, another Midwesterner who fled in order to create himself elsewhere (Paris, Spain, Cuba, Africa, Italy) and become the great writer as celebrity and performing artist.

And Donald Trump invented Donald Trump. Who is to say that he overdid it? The invention carried him very far.

17

F. Scott Fitzgerald wrote this epigraph for *The Great Gatsby*:

> Then wear the gold hat, if that will move her;
> If you can bounce high, bounce for her, too;
> Till she cry, "Lover, gold-hatted, high-bouncing lover,
> I must have you!"

Fitzgerald had a way with what he called "gestures of personality"—and an ineffable touch when he dreamed of money and spun out its emotional aesthetics. He endowed money with an atmosphere of longing and chivalry and the lost cause.

In a short story called "The Rich Boy," one of Fitzgerald's characters says, "Let me tell you about the very rich. They are different from you and me."

It became a famous American formula.

Ernest Hemingway, who was unaccountably vicious in his dealings with Fitzgerald, picked up the line and used it in his story called "The Snows of Kilimanjaro," referring to Fitzgerald as "poor Julian" and implying that he himself was the "someone" with the snappy reply: "He remembered poor Julian and his romantic awe of [the rich] and how he had started a story once that began, 'The very rich are different from you and me.' And how someone had said to Julian, 'Yes, they have more money.'"

The exchange never occurred as an actual conversation between the two men. In his biography of Maxwell Perkins, A. Scott Berg relates that one day in 1936 Hemingway had lunch with Perkins—who was his and Fitzgerald's editor—and the critic Mary Colum. Hemingway remarked, "I am getting to know the rich." Colum replied, "The only difference between the rich and other people is that the rich have more money."

In "The Snows of Kilimanjaro," Hemingway credited himself with that nice deadpan deflation. It was another in a string of his sneering denigrations of Fitzgerald, who, back in the 1920s, had befriended and encouraged Hemingway and had made the mistake of confiding in him and trying to be his friend.

Would it have been interesting if he chose to say, "The very *poor* are different from you and me"? Would it have been truer?

The country's founding idea of being both prosperous and virtuous, a partner of God, or at least a protégé—of doing well and doing good, in America's optative win-win ideology of itself—posed questions about the moral worth of the rich. Despite what Christ had to say about them, the poor have never counted for much in America, except as sentimental characters adduced in political arguments (in *Uncle Tom's Cabin* or *The Grapes of Wrath*, say).

The nation's founding Christianity was burdened—even embarrassed—by Christ's preference for the very poor and abhorrence of the rich. It was the poor who would inherit the Kingdom of Heaven.

But I am not sure that the country ever took Jesus Christ seriously on that point. Poverty meant abjection, and who wanted an abject America? The credibility of the literal Kingdom of Heaven waned; or else, as a practical matter (in the teachings of the social gospel that came in with such theologians as Walter Rauschenbusch), the Kingdom of Heaven came to be reimagined as an earthly goal, a destination that would be reached not in eternity but in history, as society improved itself.

Henry Luce, the founder of *TIME* and *Life* magazines, and the son of China missionaries, said he hoped that America would become the world's "first humane, prosperous, technological, and reverent civilization." Those four adjectives (humane, prosperous, technological, reverent) managed neatly to consolidate the four points of the American compass: the material and the spiritual, the past and the future.

There is not much evidence in history, however, that America ever allowed the Mount of Olives to inhibit the pursuit of wealth.

When Fitzgerald said, "The very rich are different from you and me," he did not mean to suggest that "you and me" are poor. Rather, he seemed to assume that "you and me" are creatures of the great American middle.

From the perspective of the provincial American norm (whether in Oak Park, Illinois, where Hemingway grew up, or in Fitzgerald's Minneapolis), great wealth was as fanciful as El Dorado, the mystical stuff of dreams. Dorothy's Kansas was not poor by any means, but it was ordinary, black and white. Oz, like Fitzgerald's imagined world of money, was alive with bright colors, with Technicolor as gaudy and opulent as Gatsby's silk shirts, the ones that cause Daisy to weep, overcome by emotions of magnificence, of gorgeous amplitude.

Hemingway said his object was to create "one true sentence." He was, however, somewhat dishonest on the subject of wealth and poverty as they touched his life. On many other subjects, he was simply a tremendous liar.

After he had left his first wife, Hadley, and his young son and gone off to marry Pauline Pfeiffer in 1926, he assuaged his guilt by elaborating a myth of the happy poverty that he had enjoyed with his first wife when they lived in rooms above the sawmill in Paris (a life humble and good and clean and authentic—virtuous) and of the perfidy of the moneyed people (Pauline's family back in Piggott, Arkansas, had money). These people included friends like Gerald and Sarah Murphy and their crowd on the French Riviera, who had lured him, in his gifted and shining naïveté, away from his happy home. By the time Hemingway came to write "The Snows of Kilimanjaro" in the mid-1930s, the marinade of alcohol and self-pity had done damage to his brain and to his moral perspectives. His alter ego in the story, a writer named Harry, is dying of an infection—gangrene. Vultures loiter on the margins of the camp. A hyena lurks in the shadows. The rot of the gangrene stinks.

Wealth, you see, was the gangrene, the fatal toxin—faithlessness causes decay. But Hemingway deflected his guilt and laid it bitterly upon the rich.

The theme of virtuous poverty—which meant to him the integrity of his artistic gift before it became poisoned—and the theme of treacherous wealth would stew for years and emerge in *A Moveable Feast*, a lovely, translucent, and yet intermittently nasty piece of work that is the full blossoming of Hemingway's money myth. *A Moveable Feast* was published posthumously, in 1964. It amounted to Hemingway's lyric calculation of just how much other people's wealth had cost him.

Hemingway was contemptuous of Fitzgerald in part because Fitzgerald was so smitten by the ways of the rich. Hemingway mythologized money as evil, or something like evil, while Fitzgerald mythologized it as a doomed but enchanted fairyland.

In matters of bragging and lying and self-exoneration, Hemingway bore a resemblance to Donald Trump. Both men have been American originals and American types. Both have insisted on being the center of attention. Both have had a genius for publicity, self-presentation, and self-mythologizing.

Both have been great apes, like the dominant males in *Tarzan of the Apes*—uprooters of trees, chest pounders. Hemingway was a ferocious liar and invented heroic and even murderous roles for himself—claiming, for example, to have fought with the Arditi during the Great War in Italy, when, in reality, he had only been an ambulance driver.

Hemingway's biographer Mary V. Dearborn wrote: "To the Hemingway family, [Ernest] claimed not only to have joined in that battle [at Vittorio Veneto] but to have been awarded the 'Croix d'Guerre or Croce D'Guerra' for his actions there, a lie told with so little regard for being found out that his motivations seem downright bizarre."

Hemingway spent only seven months in Italy and four days in combat, and yet his experience there, which of course included the serious shrapnel wound, became the foundation of the Hemingway myth and cult and oeuvre—war, death, disillusion—and, after his youth in the Great War, that expert, sophisticated tourism that made him "Papa" to his courtiers and a dominant male in Italy, Paris, Spain, Key West, Cuba, and Africa. Hemingway would tell and retell the story of his wounding, "often fictitiously, trying out scenarios of heroism."

Hemingway claimed to know everything about everything—fishing, hunting, bullfighting, food, wine, war—and, often enough, he did. One of his attractive qualities was his reverence for knowledge and competence.

He spoke often of doing things "truly." The adverb became, at last, an absurdity of his style, as when, in *Across the River and into the Trees*, he described the young Italian countess, Renata, when she dines with the old beat-up Colonel Cantwell, as chewing her steak "well and truly."

For all his use of the word "true," Hemingway's life was filled with lies—the lies he told habitually, lies as self-embellishments, and lies as self-glorifications, as if the truth was seldom sufficient in itself, at first glance, but had to be sought in all possible variations of what might be or might have been. Thucydides (the cofounder of written history, and of journalism, too) believed in telling only what he knew to be true. Herodotus (the other cofounder) told not only what he knew to be true but also what people believed to be true: their lies and superstitions and dreams and customs, however irrational. Hemingway claimed to be a Thucydides man (only the truth, only the known facts), but as myth-maker he was all Herodotus: He was a culture unto himself, with his own codes of behavior, his own language ("What's the gen?"; "Ballroom bananas"; "How do you like it now, gentlemen?") and superstitions, and his own multiple versions of everything that happened to him.

Hemingway committed suicide, as his father had before him. Suicide is a corollary of self-obsession—a natural denouement, narcissism gone into a new dimension. But that's unfair. His brain was damaged and he knew it. He could not work, or think straight. He took the Roman's way out. That, too, is true.

One may admire and loathe Hemingway at the same time—such contradictions are easily accommodated among the American binaries.

Hemingway had many friends, and a great gift of friendship, but he tended to be treacherous, especially to those to whom he was indebted. A perverse malice welled up within him—an irrational ingratitude. There are many examples of people who helped and befriended him, and whom he responded to in this way: Sherwood Anderson (whom he viciously satirized in *The Torrents of Spring*); Ford Madox Ford (a superb writer whom Hemingway mocked); Gertrude Stein (a close friend of the writer's in Paris who taught him a great deal and helped him invent the Hemingway style); Scott Fitzgerald; and others. He turned on them, maybe in the same way he turned on his mother, whom he quite convincingly claimed to hate. There was something in this of the dog that guards his lamb chop and growls and snaps and grows prehistoric and threatens to devour the person who gave it to him.

Emerson said that every hero becomes a bore at last. In Hemingway and Fitzgerald, the 20th century gave us two of them, I'm afraid. Is this also true of America? Has America itself become a bore at last?

18

The American elegists play the cello and the violin. The boosters play the brass instruments.

The elegists favor the note of threnody and decline and loss—a falling off from a better but irretrievable past. Elegy is characteristically an intellectual's note, since something in the very process of reflection and writing—the processing of experience through writing, life recollected in tranquility—establishes a connection of experience with longing and regret. Writing draws from memory and memory is of things past, and, writing therefore has a tendency toward regret and loss. Is that true? The elegists savor—they take an almost physical pleasure in—the poignance of loss. As W. B. Yeats wrote in a poem that introduced a book of Irish short stories, "The saddest chimes are best enjoyed."

The boosters tend toward boisterous and even vulgar activism—the crass application of intelligence and energy to the material future. Donald Trump stands as a representative of the type.

The distinction between the elegists and the boosters is useful in describing the gap between intellectuals and businesspeople.

Edmund Wilson can serve as a case study. A friend of Scott Fitzgerald's from their days at Princeton, an important literary and social critic from the 1920s to the 1960s, and someone who was often described as "America's last man of letters," Wilson, like other intellectuals of the time, inclined toward elegy and nostalgia. But like other intellectuals, under the pressure of the 1929 crash and the Depression, Wilson transformed his nostalgia into utopianism: into a radical social vision, communism, that would break up the intolerable and failed (so it seemed at the time) capitalist present. Communism would usher in a new society and restore the principle of justice that, in the minds of elegists, had been ruined by capitalism and its "contradictions." Wilson wrote much excellent leftist reportage in the late twenties and thirties—covering the bitter coal miners' strike in Harlan County, Kentucky, for example—for the *New Republic*, where he was literary editor. In 1940, he published *To the Finland Station,* an epic but starry-eyed parsing of the origins of socialism and Soviet communism. Admiring Lenin, Wilson forgave far too much. Years later, in the 1950s, when Lenin's and Stalin's crimes became clearer to him, along with the totalitarian nature of the Communist regimes, he wrote a new introduction to the work and acknowledged its naïveté. That was as far as Wilson would go in becoming a booster.

The Communists and Socialists in the New Deal were American elegists who had been energized by the idea that the crisis in capitalism had opened the door to an ideal new day. Communism was their version of the Kingdom of Heaven (always look for the religious thread in American political life). Communist or Christian, it was a matter of faith or, if you prefer, magic thinking. The great malignant machine of capitalism had broken down and the elegists, now gone fervent and ideological (elegiac intellectuals adore an ideology), thought that in the future the people could go on entirely without the great machine, sustained instead by an all-powerful and presumably just and righteous government.

A more poignant, complex case may be examined in Whittaker Chambers. In his youth, Chambers became a Communist, and by and by, a Soviet agent. He was an accomplished intellectual—one of many of the type—seduced into a life of action by a vision of virtue that would override all contradictions, by a force of will, and, where necessary, by ruthless violence. A just society might be achieved by acts of extreme (but necessary) injustice.

After the Hiss case was over, Chambers wrote a memoir and apologia called *Witness,* whose opening chapter, about his miserable boyhood in a more or less psychotic household on Long Island—where his crazy grandmother wandered the rooms at night with a butcher knife, and his beloved brother committed suicide by sticking his head in a gas oven—is one of the most brilliant and eloquently doomy items of American elegy ever written. It is the Fall of the House of Chambers.

Chambers—a melodramatic man who carried a pistol at times and in restaurants sat with his back to the wall—worked for the Communists through the thirties, with Alger Hiss and others in the New Deal, filching inside information from the US Government and passing it on to Moscow. Chambers eventually had a change of mind and heart—at around the same time that my then-teenage mother did, actually—and left the party, just as she had done.

He went to work at *TIME* and became one of Henry Luce's favorite writers. Now he played his doomy cello (his prose sounded like Elgar's *Cello Concerto*) in the boosters' cause. He wrote like Jeremiah. In 1948, he testified before the House Un-American Activities Committee, identifying Alger Hiss as a Communist. It became one of the defining American dramas, like Sacco and Vanzetti or the Scopes Monkey Trial in Tennessee.

Alger Hiss, something of a darling and hero of the elites, had moved in the highest circles of the American government during the New Deal and the war. He was instrumental in founding the United Nations. He had the Establishment connections. Secretary of State Dean Acheson said, "I will not turn my back on Alger Hiss." John Foster Dulles gave him a character reference. In 1948 and for a time thereafter, Hiss was the Fred Astaire of the drama (slim, debonair, sophisticated) and Chambers, a heavy, disheveled man with bad teeth and an unpleasantly covert air, looked like Fatty Arbuckle as imagined by a Russian novelist.

Ultimately, the case became an American sermon on how appearances may deceive. Chambers had told the truth about Hiss, who eventually went to prison for forty-four months. After that, he spent the rest of his life selling stationery in Greenwich Village. He never admitted his guilt.

When Saul Bellow and I were professors at Boston University in the early 2000s, he told me a story about *TIME* magazine, Chambers, and the Depression. Hard up for money, Bellow approached his friend James Agee, who worked for the magazine, and asked for help in getting a job there. Agee seemed a little exasperated (lots of writers in the Village were after him with the same request), but he fixed it up for Bellow to come to the *TIME* offices to speak with a back-of-the-book editor named Whittaker Chambers.

Bellow appeared at Chambers's office on the appointed day. Chambers had his back turned and was staring out the window. After a long moment, he swiveled around in his chair and demanded, "Young man, who was John Keats?"

Bellow, bewildered by what seemed a trick question, or at least a weird one, tried to figure out the proper answer and replied: "A poet?"

Chambers, stern and surly, growled: "What kind of poet?"

"An English poet?"

"Yeah. What else?"

"A romantic English poet, early 19th century?"

Chambers waved his hand in dismissal: "Sorry. You have no place at *TIME* magazine."

He swiveled his chair back around to the window. The interview was over.

Bellow left in mystification. Years later, he was talking to the poet John Berryman, who told him he had had exactly the same experience with Chambers at *TIME*. Only in Berryman's case, the question was about Samuel Taylor Coleridge.

Bellow and Berryman decided that Agee and Chambers, who were friends (which was not as unlikely a friendship as it might seem at first glance) had made a deal that when Agee's friends importuned him for a job at the magazine, Chambers would get rid of them so that Agee could claim he had done his best by his indigent buddies.

Chambers never became a booster, even though he played for the boosters' team. He was on their side as Henry Luce's court prophet. Chambers wrote elegies for capitalism—he called it "the losing side." His mind was grooved to lamentations. He wrote about the destruction of the West in tones of exalted misery—as if he were mourning the destruction of the Second Temple: *By the rivers of Babylon, there we sat down, yea, we wept, when we remembered Zion.*

The "mishkid" side of Luce, raised on biblical alarms, admired Chambers's performances. On the other hand, Luce was also unmistakably an American booster, and had been since he was a child, at his parents' Presbyterian mission in Shandong. His father, the reverend Henry Winters Luce, crackled with ideas and "pep," one of his favorite words, and told his children, "Use your native Lucepower!" They started the day at the mission with cold baths at 6 a.m. Reverend Luce became one of the Presbyterians' most effective fundraisers, and was frequently called back to America to haunt the offices of rich, successful Christians and persuade them to make some of their money virtuous by supporting the missions. One of the his most ardent supporters was Nettie McCormick, the widow of Cyrus McCormick, who actually tried to adopt young Henry Luce and raise him in Chicago. The offer scared little Harry to death and fortunately his parents politely declined the offer.

In the mind of elegiac intellectuals, businessmen (they were always men) were crude, venal, dull, unimaginative, philistine, and overmasculine—"bourgeois," oafish, insensitive. Woodrow Wilson, an academic of genteel Confederate background, born and raised in the South, became the president of Princeton University at the beginning of the 20th century, at around the same time that the Progressive movement got started, with the idea of reforming business and government and driving the money-changers and plutocrats from the American temple. Wilson declared that his mission as Princeton's president was to see to it that by the time a student of his graduated, he shared none of his father's opinions—about anything.

There must be, in other words, a genteel, civilized repudiation of the morals and standards of the fathers, many of whom were businessmen of the Gilded Age. It should have been, if you think about it, an extraordinary thing for a college president to announce it as his mission to persuade his students to turn their backs on their own parents' values and ways of looking at the world. Parents in the 21st century, however, will recognize this pattern of ideological subversion in a new generation of progressive academics.

19

I came across the story of William Keyser by chance. The more I learned about him, the more he seemed admirable to me—a man of business and a paragon in a corrupt age.

William Keyser died in 1904, having lived long enough to see the transition from the Gilded Age to the age of progressivism and reform—the time of Teddy Roosevelt, the muckraking *McClure's*, Ida Tarbell, and Lincoln Steffens. Keyser's career was long and prosperous and, unlike those of Jay Gould and other capos of the Gilded Age, had about it the atmosphere of doing well and doing good and thinking constructively in the long term. He was the sort of man whose life and character Americans might cite when they wished to reassure themselves about the stability of their own virtue. He was what an old-fashioned father ought to be: sane, thoughtful, provident. Good. He would have been cast as the father if 19th-century America had been a situation comedy.

He was involved in several lines of work in his sixty-nine years. He started in the iron ore business in Baltimore, where he was born. Then he became vice president of Baltimore and Ohio Railroad—Baltimore's great hope to compete with the Erie Canal in gaining access to the Mississippi and the West. The work affected his health and he declined an invitation to become president of B&O. According to his great-granddaughter Louise Bruce, who supervised the publication of his memoirs, "Keyser next engaged in mining copper near Globe, Arizona. . . . Subsequently, he signed a contract for the shipment to Baltimore of the copper ore output from the rich Anaconda Mine near Helena, Montana. The ore came east for smelting at the Keyser-owned company, the Canton Copper Works."

He did well. He did good. He helped Johns Hopkins University acquire the land for its vastly expanded Homewood campus. The Keyser Quadrangle at the university honors his work. He did other things. In retirement, he built All Souls Church in Reisterstown outside Baltimore, a small Episcopal church he constructed in memory of his mother, Elizabeth Wyman Keyser.

Keyser's life upheld the notion of the civilized man of character and balance. The 20th century did what it could to discredit the model. The 21st century has all but completed the demolition. The precedent of the well-upholstered and virtuous William Keyser is an anachronism to which I revert wistfully.

He gave his memoir the modest title *Recollections of a Busy Life*, and began the book with a long view that ventured onto the dangerous ground of hereditary merit:

> Observation has convinced me that there is more in heredity than we generally suppose, and that family traits, both mental and physical, descend from generation to generation, having more or less influence, even if not always discernible, serving to mold the character and shape the actions.

He continued:

> Success or failure, viewed from this standpoint, will assume an altogether different aspect, and whether we look upon life's results as the one or the other, our individual part in working it out will appear as secondary and subordinate, not paramount and controlling. I do not for one moment mean by this, that individual effort and personal qualities have not much to do in the achievement of results and in securing success; on the contrary I fully realize that these are the important factors; but that either or both can command success, experience only clearly demonstrates is not always the case. . . .
>
> Life, as experience teaches, is very complex and many sided; it is the here and the hereafter—this present distance and that which is

to follow—and touches not only self, but our relation to others, our duty to God as well as to ourselves and our neighbor.

The 20th century was inclined to treat such thoughts, especially when coming from a wealthy man, as bromides touching on the racist in their assumptions. Either a wealthy man was assumed to be speaking hypocritically (as if to disguise the bad motives, the chicanery, and the greed that had enabled him to acquire his wealth) or else he was accorded an impure admiration, a starry-eyed envy. It was hard to think that a man like William Keyser (a capitalist, titan, manager, a powerful man in his world) might be an admirable figure and even a hero.

Let me veer away for a moment to visit an adjacent character—Horatio Alger.

If Balzac said great money comes from great crime, Alger's tales proposed the opposite idea: that, in America, success is the natural result of virtue—of purity of heart, of a radiant, steadfast character. What Alger meant was: If you are good, you will do well, and being rich and good (which is a different thing from being good and rich), you will fulfill the national destiny and justify the tremendous trust that God reposed in the American project.

Actually, Alger's books (some 120 volumes of young adult fiction turned out in the Gilded Age) did not lift the heroes (Ragged Dick and the others) from "rags to riches," but rather from poverty to a respectable life in the middle and upper middle class. Alger's hero, starting often as a child of the streets, arrived, by luck and good character and perhaps by the chance help of a benign wealthy uncle figure, at a solid, Victorian gentility. William Keyser would have been such an uncle.

Alger's tales amounted to a response to Christ's parables (warnings about the camel and the eye of the needle, and so on): Whatever facts might suggest otherwise at the time that he wrote his tales (brutal economic dislocations of the Gilded Age, labor/management violence), Alger preached a sweet, providential vision of American life. Success was entirely compatible with virtue—in Keyser's message, as well. Virtue and success were reconciled in Alger's influential tales. Virtue enabled wealth, almost guaranteed it. It was pretty to think so.

The idea of virtue producing money offered America's solution to the conundrum of works vs. grace—the Calvinist idea that nothing one might do in the way of good deeds (or good business) will necessarily bring salvation (God made up his mind about you and me long ago, and for all eternity).

The 20th century read Horatio Alger in a spirit of amusement and wonder at the naïveté of the Boy Scout Dudley Doright, or the spirit of Dink Stover, a quality that might be endearing or might be sinister, depending. The side of the 20th-century mind that was shaped by Freud and Lytton Strachey and their knowingness about humans' hidden motives would be apt to pry into Alger's own biography and find concealed, besmirching (to some eyes) evidence of, for example, homosexuality.

Capitalism and corruption and the piracies of the Gilded Age had done more than enough to discredit themselves, and such sagas had the effect not only of tarnishing big money but also, it seemed, of foreclosing the possibility that decent, constructive energies might still be at work among plutocrats.

Where Keyser's mind sought to resurrect old gods, Freud was a powerful new secular prophet of the 20th century, and yet many of the intellectual premises of the 20th century itself would eventually come to seem provincial, naïve, and temporary. The century was full of transient but devastating ideas, lethal waves of political fashion—Nazism, fascism, communism, Bolshevism, Maoism—that killed millions of people and then receded.

Keyser's mind had the virtue of refusing to get carried away. I liked his Victorian prose and circumspection, his benevolent clichés:

> The inheritance of wealth often proves a curse rather than a blessing.
> Many a fine character blighted by the possession, has lost its manly
> qualities; and many a bright and gifted mind, under the same baleful
> influence, has parted with its integrity and gone out in darkness. If
> used and valued aright it is one of the greatest and most properly
> coveted of blessings, bringing as it does, with great responsibilities,
> even greater opportunities.

Keyser stood for the idea that these things, once true, ought to be true again. I thought of him in connection with midcoast American Quakers, frequently gifted businessmen, who may have been illuminated by the Inner Light and may have been sweet in their contemplations, yet were known for sharp dealing; they did very well.

❧

Johns Hopkins was born in Maryland in 1795 into a privileged Quaker family of plantation owners. His father freed his slaves (as many Quakers did), and so, as a teenager, Johns was obliged to interrupt his education and come home to work on the plantation, doing the work that previously had been done by slaves. When he was seventeen, his parents sent him to Baltimore to work for an uncle, Gerard Hopkins, a wholesale grocer and commission merchant, who had a daughter named Elizabeth.

In time, Johns and Elizabeth fell in love and they hoped to be married. But they were first cousins. The Society of Friends forbade the marriage of first cousins—"a prudent genetic policy," said one Quaker history, "especially for a society whose members at that time only approved marriage between members of the Society." By contrast, a European family of infinitely greater wealth, the Rothschilds, encouraged the marrying of first cousins, considering that the practice enhanced family solidarity and guaranteed the secrecy of its far-flung international operations.

After being refused, the young couple, Johns and Elizabeth, waited for a year. Then they again asked the Meeting for permission to marry. Again, they were refused.

And so they abandoned the hope of marriage. Neither of them ever married. Johns Hopkins devoted himself to his business, that of a commission merchant, and in time he amassed a fortune. He provided a house for Elizabeth at the corner of St. Paul and Franklin streets in Baltimore, he gave her financial security, and in his will, he provided for her brothers and sisters as well.

It was that famous will that would also leave the funds—$7 million (to the amazement of the city of Baltimore)—to start Johns Hopkins

University and the teaching hospital. Hopkins left other bequests for institutions benefitting the poor, especially African American children.

Hopkins's record as a Quaker had a minor blemish. In 1826, he was read out of the Lombard Street Meeting for trading in whiskey. He was a stubborn man. Others had been reprimanded by the Meeting on the same grounds, but they had apologized and stopped selling whiskey, and so had been allowed to rejoin the Meeting. Hopkins refused. Selling whiskey was good business and earned him a profit, and he was single-minded about making a profit. Later, he mellowed, and he regretted his stubbornness and admitted that he had made a mistake.

The Baltimore Yearly Meeting's 1806 Book of Discipline—a manual, updated annually, that summarized the consensus of the Friends' thinking—addressed the matter of how to conduct business: "We do not condemn industry," it said, "we believe it to be not only praise-worthy but indispensable."

So the Quakers aligned themselves, here anyway, with Cotton Mather's idea of rowing to heaven with two oars. (In point of doctrine, Puritans hated Quakers, whom they regarded as "crazy fanatics." The Puritans under Governor John Endecott persecuted Quakers and actually executed three of them.) But Friends were counseled to be careful to undertake no business beyond what they understood or had the resources to conduct well and properly.

The Book of Discipline advised avoiding risky enterprises. Businesspeople should engage in frequent and thorough accounting practices; should avoid paper credit (which involved "endorsements, to give it an appearance of value, without an intrinsic reality"); and should be cautious of partnerships with others.

If an enterprise should fail, Quaker businesspeople should immediately report its demise to the Meeting. They were advised not to favor one creditor over another in making restitution and to give repayment of debt priority over donations to the Meeting.

"It is the affectionate desire of the Yearly Meeting," said the Book's section on trade, "that Friends may wait for divine counsel in all their engagements, and not suffer their minds to be carried away by an inordinate desire of worldly riches."

The Quaker Book of Discipline was consistent with, for example, Buddhist teachings on the subject of virtue and money and "rightful means," which concerned any occupation that did not cause unnecessary harm to other living things. A book discussing the Buddha's teaching on prosperity stated, "The layperson's objective [is to] live a long and dignified life through rightful means." Such teachings, whether Quaker or Buddhist, sought to warn money away from its uglier, and no doubt inherent, tendency toward selfishness, ostentation, and power. The Buddha said, "A lay follower should not engage in five types of business.... Business in weapons, business in human beings, business in meat, business in intoxicants, and business in poison."

A mid-Atlantic Quaker composite formed the portrait of Theodore Dreiser's fictional banker Solon Barnes, depicted in the author's last novel, *The Bulwark,* published posthumously in 1946. Dreiser's research for the novel—a multigenerational saga in which the children of the righteous father, Solon Barnes, stray into vice and error, secularism, and unbelief in the early 20th century—involved studying the histories of Quaker families, and he sometimes used surnames that he borrowed from their family trees.

It was Quakers who settled Nantucket, and Quakers (Captains Peleg and Bildad) who owned the fictional captain Ahab's fatal ship, the *Pequod.* Hetty Green, the "richest woman in America" in the late 19th century, who in turn became a legend, also emerged from Quaker stock, in New Bedford, Massachusetts.

Hetty Green (1834–1916) is worth another digression. She became "the Witch of Wall Street": the world's richest woman in the late 19th and early 20th centuries. She was famous for a Scrooge-like stinginess (she did her work at a desk in the lobby of a bank in order to avoid paying office rent) and for a shrewd, masculine style of financial investment. America knew her—unfairly—as a hard, ruthless, unfeeling woman, an image that contradicted the 19th-century feminine ideal of warmth, domesticity, and compassion. Detesting publicity, she lived in hotels or rented rooms, and would move to new quarters the minute someone in the building found out who she was. When she died, she was worth about $4 billion in today's dollars.

A century after Green's death, Oprah Winfrey, born black and poor in rural Mississippi in 1954, amassed an equivalent fortune. She has been said to be the richest woman in America.

Green and Winfrey—both of them American, both women, both equivalently rich—are opposites in almost every respect.

Winfrey became a phenomenon, a world celebrity. Tabloids for years followed the ups and downs of her love life and her weight. Covers of her extraordinarily successful *O* magazine image show the face of Oprah in its many moods and guises. Where Green was private and reclusive, Winfrey built an immense public career, and a fortune, by minutely examining and exploiting her own private life and the private lives of others in formats of public confession. Where Green was grimly covert, Winfrey was gushingly, sentimentally overt.

The lives of Hetty and Oprah are one measure of the distance America has traveled. The country's public and private dimensions have been conflated, as have its sexual roles and expectations. If—whatever the particular facts of each case—men and women, and blacks and whites as well, are presumed to be equal in the professions, in business, in the military, and in other areas, then the dimensions of the public and private are also presumed to have equal rights and claims and powers, as it were: The public and the private have equal validity and legitimacy in the scheme of things. Freud's insight into the immense potency of intimate circumstances was a precursor to Oprah's blossoming success. She would make a great fortune practicing spontaneous moral psychiatry—performance psychiatry—before millions of viewers.

William Keyser was born in Baltimore. His family was not Quaker but Episcopalian.

Keyser recorded that "my first commercial venture was rather unique." He had stolen one of his mother's gold chains from her bureau drawer and sold it for a small sum to a jeweler; then he used some of the money to buy cheap cinnamon-flavored cigars at a shop on Pratt Street: "These were a favorite article of luxury or as it proved in my case, of debauch."

Baltimore was still a small town then, and the jeweler called at the house that evening and returned the gold chain. The boy was put to bed with nothing more traumatic than a lecture from his mother, but he claimed it was so effective that he decided then and there to live an honest life. And he proceeded to do so.

᳹

Jean Strouse, author of a fine biography of J. P. Morgan, also wrote a book called *Alice James*, about the sister of Henry and William James. All four of her characters—the iconic American financier J. P. Morgan, on the one hand, and the James siblings (Henry James, the novelist; William James, the philosopher; and Alice James, the gifted, mysterious neurotic), on the other—were creatures of the 19th century. Strouse set the money people and the intellectual people—two different universes—side by side because she was interested in the way that they thought about each other. She touched a Henry Jamesian nerve in doing so: "Interesting perceptions are preferable to marketable achievements only when there is enough money to go around." It was a perfectly American thing to say: Business—money—must take precedence over the play of the mind. But that formulation is always construed—by intellectuals anyway—to be definitive evidence of an incurable anti-intellectualism in the American scheme of things.

That is another of the great binaries—the businesspeople and the intellectuals.

Henry Luce from time to time would complain that American novelists never made businessmen their heroes. Sinclair Lewis first wrote *Main Street* (1920) and *Babbitt* (1922), and then in 1929 published *Dodsworth*: Sam Dodsworth was an American hero, a kind of visionary car manufacturer. Babbitt was an American boob, a chiseler in his business and practically a moron in his consumer appetites. Lewis lavished contempt on poor George Babbitt for his tiled bathroom with its nickel fixtures, his pretentious hunting prints on the wall, and his "grenadier and-irons...like samples in a shop, desolate, unwanted. Lifeless things of commerce." Lewis was working a vein of American self-reproach that

Mencken, Sherwood Anderson, Edgar Lee Masters, Edward Arlington Robinson, and others had explored, and that would continue to be rich in American lore through later books like Grace Metalious's *Peyton Place*: the small town as whited sepulchre, as microcosmic repository of all human vices, hypocritically concealed by the facades of Rotary, the Chamber of Commerce, the Elks, and the Presbyterian church: Narrowness, hypocrisy, and intolerance were the small-town sins, worse in a metaphysical way than the specific hidden dramas of, say, drunkenness and incest: Here the honest mind could only be profoundly lonely, isolated. Here the honest mind dreamed only of escape. How to get out? How to get out?

Richard Nixon said that as a boy in Whittier, California, he heard the train whistle and dreamed of escape.

The events of 2020—the pandemic, the lockdowns, the racial disturbances—have abruptly reversed the flow. It is the big cities that people now wish to escape.

Luce's critics thought that the publisher was a booster of the Babbitt America. It would be more accurate to say that Luce in his philosophy supported the Dodsworth America (he founded *Fortune* magazine to appeal to the Dodsworths of the country) but that his magazine empire also depended heavily for its livelihood upon the consumer appetites of the Babbitts. Henry Winters Luce and Elizabeth Root Luce, the publisher's admirable missionary parents—selfless, intelligent people, austere in their ways, almost too good to be true—would gently reprove their son for the kinds of ads he took for his magazines, especially the ads for cigarettes and liquor.

In the Babbitt-Dodsworth dichotomy lies an important difference—all the difference in the world: two distinct ways of looking at American money enterprises.

The Babbitt America was stupid, venal, corrupt, and provincial, while the Dodsworth America was energetic, able, productive, and admirable, even heroic.

Luce was entirely dedicated to the idea of Dodsworth America, although he frequently criticized it. Sinclair Lewis came around slowly to seeing the virtues of that America. It was Dodsworth's America that won World War II—the industrial might created by American industry.

In one way of looking at it, the New Deal was a temporizing, inefficient exercise that distracted the American people until the war came along to rescue the American economy.

❧

William James sometimes played golf with John D. Rockefeller, but there was no meeting of minds, and James called him "a man ten stories deep, and to me quite unfathomable." Rockefeller might have said the same thing about the Harvard philosopher. Money and literary intellect would evolve into feuding parallel cultures—like the Hatfields and McCoys. Each would resent and sometimes detest the other. They were apples and oranges, cats and dogs. They stopped playing golf together or intermarrying. The novelist Ford Madox Ford, a relentlessly literary man, wrote that the commercial civilization "could not possibly produce a great man since it [has] so little to express that its expression could not possibly lead to greatness."

Each found the other "unfathomable." T. S. Eliot had a roommate at Harvard who after graduation went to work on Wall Street. When "The Waste Land" was published in 1922, Eliot's ex-roommate bought a copy and started reading it on the way to work. He was so incensed by Tom Eliot's modernist obscurities that he threw the book out the window of his commuter train.

By the time the 20th century rumbled onstage, large, primitive forces of money and ideology were colliding with each other worldwide (capitalism with its booms and depressions; and the violent variations on communism, fascism, and other ideological systems). As the century proceeded, the conflicts became rhythmic, tidal, and, from time to time, apocalyptic. The American feud became ferocious and decisive during the New Deal. Many of America's culture wars emerged from that time.

But in America long ago, Ralph Waldo Emerson had managed in his sweet way to close the gap, if only for a moment. He was an intellectual character and a hero of intellectuals—the wonder rabbi of the WASPs. But also, rather strangely, he would become the patron saint of the American entrepreneur—an inspiration, especially in his essay

"Self-Reliance," to the thoughtful type for whom the idea of America as a "business civilization" was not a contradiction in terms. Walt Whitman also said complimentary things about business enterprise: Business, wrote the poet of American democracy, was "an immense and noble attribute of man ... the tie and interchange of all the peoples of the earth."

&

Henry Adams, the most thoroughgoing of all American elegists, lamented the waning of his dynasty that had given the country two presidents, John Adams and John Quincy Adams. He claimed, with elegant rue, that he inhabited the 18th century and that he abhorred everything that came later. He lived through the Civil War (spending the war in London as secretary to his father, Charles Francis Adams, US minister to the Court of St. James's), through the Gilded Age, and into the time of Teddy Roosevelt (his friend), the Progressive movement, and America's accession to world power.

Ironic elegy was the Henry Adams note, which deepened and grew more authentic after his wife, Clover Adams, committed suicide in their house on Lafayette Square, across from the White House.

Adams was a wealthy man in the Gilded Age—his brother was president of the Union Pacific Railroad—who at the same time managed to reprehend the wealthy, the Malefactors of Great Wealth, and the (as he thought) sad decline that Ulysses Grant represented in the American presidency and American life. He joked that in order to disprove Darwin, one had only to observe the evident devolution from George Washington to Grant. (From the racial point of view of the 21st century, Grant in fact had been a considerable improvement upon the slave owner Washington.)

The split between elegists and boosters is a fundamental in the story of America and its money. The elegists always take the boosters to be vulgarians, lacking brains or, anyway, refinement.

The 1952 presidential race between Adlai Stevenson and Dwight Eisenhower was a classic enactment of the split. In those days, the American divisions were muted by postwar prosperity and domesticity, but, at the same time, inflamed by McCarthyism. Stevenson was called

an "egghead," even though he was not, in truth, much of an intellectual. The elegant speeches for which he became noted were written for
him by people like Arthur Schlesinger Jr. and John Kenneth Galbraith.
Eisenhower, after a lifetime on army posts, had fallen in with prospering
Republicans who were boosters in a corporate and country club sort of
way. Cerebrotonic Adlai and his people shuddered at Ike's golfing and
his reading of Zane Grey Westerns, but the general won in a landslide,
and then repeated the victory in 1956.

20

For a long time, America and China have talked to each other somewhat obscurely, tapping through the earth, exchanging mutually uncomprehending ideals. They continue to do this in the 21st century.

Babbitt, Sinclair Lewis's 1922 satire, starts with Babbitt dozing on his sleeping porch in Zenith and "again dreaming of the fairy child, a dream more romantic than scarlet pagodas by a silver sea." China, the other side of the world, comes to him in his dream vision, as well as the fairy girl, who is "so slim, so white, so eager." In the dream, she and Babbitt, whom she sees as young, valiant, and gallant, slip out of the house and away from his wife and friends and escape together, secretly, passionately. This furtive escape is associated with China, scarlet pagodas, and the silver sea. China, by inference, is Babbitt's Other—an exotic anti-world that is the physical and metaphysical opposite of the crass, hustling-bustling philistine American Zenith—just as, at the same time, America was an exotic anti-world to the Chinese, some of whom called it "mei guo," the beautiful country, a place of glistening perfection.

Babbitt was the parody of what Calvin Coolidge pointed to a few years later: America as a business civilization, which the intellectuals wrote off as philistine, shallow, crass.

Henry Luce—who was born in China and had no illusions about its realities (the poverty, the tendency to flood and famine and plague that might kill millions in a bad season)—idealized America, his shining birthright that all through his childhood lay on the other side of the world. He later said he wished that when someone asked him what his hometown was, he could reply, "Oskaloosa, Iowa." He dreamed now and then of being president. To him the middle-American, Rotarian view was fine. Harold Ross started the *New Yorker* in 1925, two years after *TIME* was first published, and said that his magazine was "not for the old lady in Dubuque." Luce was all in favor of the old lady in Dubuque and the rest of the family, too. He was an enthusiast of businessmen and business, up to a point anyway, and the businessman's way of looking at the world. He fretted, however, in his Presbyterian conscience—especially after World War II—about how America was to use its power and money to promote virtue in the world and advance the Kingdom of God.

Luce saw in the materialism of America not a crass, peppy Mammon-worship, but rather the continued working out of America's grace as a unique and imperfect but perfectible project, underwritten by God. Materialism could be a part of the Kingdom of God; there could be such a thing as godly materialism and godly wealth (unselfish and generous, like that of Nettie McCormick. She sent money to the far-off Chinese missionaries and built a house for the Luces there because she believed they would add a virtuous expression and purpose to her wealth. Thereby might her dollars achieve a halo).

Luce believed fervently in capitalism and a Presbyterian's God, and he considered that ideally they were both articles of the same faith. And as a missionary's son, born and raised throughout his boyhood in impoverished, turbulent China, he had a sense that material development (roads, housing, proper sanitation, and so on) was not corrupt or luxurious but rather, essential and humane. Capital and materialism, therefore, in his mind seemed perfectly compatible with Good Works and with the work of God.

Horace Greeley said, "Go West, young man," but a strong current ran the other way—flowing from America's heartland provinces toward the East, toward New York especially, and back across the Atlantic to Europe, to expatriate Paris. Malcolm Cowley emerged from around Pittsburgh; Hemingway from Oak Park, Illinois; the *New Yorker's* Harold Ross from out in Utah; Ezra Pound from Idaho; Jean Stafford from Colorado; Cole Porter from Indiana; Mary McCarthy from the Pacific Northwest;

Scott Fitzgerald and Sinclair Lewis from Minnesota; John O'Hara from Pottstown, Pennsylvania.

Henry Luce, hailing from China, migrating to Hotchkiss, Yale, and Manhattan, simply had a longer trip to make in order to arrive. He went to Oz, Manhattan, which became the seat of his magazine empire, but he cherished in his nostalgia both a mythical China and, like Dorothy, a mythical Kansas: All three of his homelands—China, Manhattan, heartland America—were ideals, creations of his moral imagination.

&

But there was another way of looking at Henry Luce. On this point, I should say a word about Pearl Buck.

The Nobel Prize–winning author Pearl S. Buck detested Luce. She attempted his literary assassination in 1949 when she published *God's Men,* a novel that portrayed Luce (called William Lane in the book) as a heartless, plutocratic press lord; oppressor; and manipulator of the Little Man. Lane (or Luce) emerged in the novel as a sexual incompetent and a clumsy sadist. Buck repeatedly informed readers that Luce-Lane had tiny hands covered with thick black hair. (In fact, Luce had long-fingered shapely hands.) Buck added that he had hair on his back. She might as well have given him a tail and horns as well.

Buck's father, Absalom Sydenstricker, was a missionary who went over to China from West Virginia. He was (unlike Luce's urbane Ivy League father, a graduate of Yale, class of 1892) a Bible-thumper with a half-mad gleam in his eye. He abandoned his wife and children for months at a time to fend for themselves in near poverty in Chinese slums while he "itinerated" in the countryside, bringing the Gospel to heathens who, for the most part, laughed at him.

Buck's novel had something of her father's fanaticism. Somewhere in the back of her mind, the resentment of her missionary childhood seems to have coalesced as hatred misdirected at Luce as a sublimated Satan; the real target of her malice may have been her own father. He was, as she admitted, a sort of backwoods Bible-crazy, while the Reverend Luce was Yale-genteel. In Buck's eyes, in any case, Harry Luce ("Boy Luce," as the Chinese servants at the mission called him) was a privileged, stuck-up little prig who did not know much about China or the Chinese language. Certainly, he did not know as much as she did, having grown up poor in the real China. She relished Chinese cooking and spoke the language perfectly with her Chinese girlfriends. She had had a Chinese lover whom she almost married. She won the Nobel Prize for her novel about Chinese peasants, *The Good Earth*.

The Luces, Pearl Buck meant to say, were drawing-room missionaries with carpets on the floor and Gibbon, Shakespeare, Dickens, and Sir Walter Scott on the bookshelves; people who held the Chinese at arm's length and, in their hearts, had never quite left Scranton. Mrs. Luce ran the Shandong household as if she were still back in her childhood home of Utica. She taught the Chinese cook to reproduce creamy, bland American dishes. Harry Luce, Buck thought, went home to America to become powerful and rich... and Republican. He turned his back on the real China, her China, and he ridiculously beatified Chiang Kai-shek and beautified the Madame, and used his sentimental, Christianizing China merely as background for his Manichaean holy war anti-communism.

The jacket copy of the Pocket Books edition of *God's Men* reads as follows: "*William Lane*—His childhood in China made him arrogant and self-centered. In America, he became the publisher of cheap tabloids which distorted the thinking of tens of millions. He believed, as he often said, that 'a man can get anything he wants as long as he is rich.'"

Here, Pearl Buck indulged herself in a complicated and (for a good American) forbidden line of civics: It was the favorite line of Luce's enemies, but it was dangerous. For the record, she and the others believed in democracy, but democracy had its limits, as when the majority happened to disagree with Buck's convictions; in such circumstances, she said that Americans, the many millions of them, were deluded. Luce's magazines, especially *TIME* and *Life*, exerted immense influence over the American mind. Could it be that Luce was correct in his opinions? Or was he, as she thought, the Prince of Lies? If so, then those millions of Americans who were his avid readers were, in effect, being seduced by the devil. America was of the people, by the people, and for the people, but on the other hand, as Luce's intellectual enemies believed, the people did not always know what was good for them. That was why they poisoned their minds by imbibing the magazines of Henry Luce.

21

On a bright summer day, I was sailing with William F. Buckley Jr. on his sloop *Patito* off the coast of Connecticut, cruising up to Maine. Bill wanted to grind in the mainsail and he asked me to hand him the winch handle. We were heeled over, and I fumbled and dropped the winch handle into the sea. There was an extra winch handle and the moment passed. But it was an expensive thing and I was chagrined by my clumsiness.

We put into Essex, Connecticut, and went to a marine supply store and Bill bought a new winch handle. I could see that it was expensive (everything on a sailboat is expensive) and I wanted to offer to pay for it. But that wouldn't do; I was his guest. It wasn't the money, anyway—Bill had money—but the clumsiness, the unsailorly fumbling. One did not lose a winch handle overboard in a stiff breeze when adjusting sail; a guy does not make such mistakes. Sailing, even of this kind (cruising with friends off the New England coast on a summer day), demanded one or two disciplined reflexes and the instinct to understand, without thinking, that a sailboat driving along in a taut wind requires a minimal precision in all hands.

There was an unstated dimension of class in these things. It was what Scott Fitzgerald was getting at, and Hemingway, too, in a different way— knowing how to sail, as it were, not losing the winch handle. *Comme il faut*. These were the preoccupations of a different world, and they seem a little preposterous now.

And so I fumbled (in a satirical, W. C. Fields kind of way, like a juggler who has lost track of a midair bowling pin—*Godfrey Daniel!*) and the bright chrome winch handle did a gleaming twirl in midair and vanished into the slapdash sea.

I looked up at Bill in embarrassed surprise. He let it go with an almost undetectable twitch of irritation (he was the politest of men) and pointed to the extra winch handle stowed nearby in a sleeve in the cockpit.

I sailed with Bill many Friday nights across the Long Island Sound to Eatons Neck. We would anchor and feast on his cook Julian's chopped eggs and caviar and filet mignon; and drink Bill's cold Chilean wine; and play poker (night baseball, high-low, everything wild); and listen to Dick Wellstood's jazz piano on the tape machine; and then strip and plunge off the stern into the cold, dark water. And so to sleep.

I remember setting off from Stamford one evening late in August, four of us on *Patito*, the wind blowing gusts of fifty miles per hour. Pat Buckley (for whom the boat was named, although she rarely came along on these sails) looked at the weather report and listened to the wind out-side the house at Wallach's Point, and said, in her drawling, melodramatic voice, "Bill, you're *insane!*" He paid no attention and we sailed across the sound in a tremendous blow—Bill at the wheel holding an old-fashioned glass filled with ice and Scotch. When we approached Eatons Neck, he sent Danny Merritt to the bow with a flashlight to peer into the wild darkness looking for the nun buoy that would guide us through the needle's eye into the cove.

"Danny," Bill called from the stern, holding the wheel with both hands but managing at the same time to brace his glass of Scotch between thumb and forefinger. "Danny, can you see the critical nun?! Can you see the critical nun!!?"

Danny found it, and with slipping and bucking gyrations, we sluiced into the cove, where suddenly all was comparatively quiet, and we dropped anchor and snugged down and dined and drank and played poker.

I never knew a man who so enjoyed his friends, his life, and of course the money, which eased the way but was not the main point of it all. Some people are stupidly rich. Bill was intelligently and generously rich.

It was a curious thing about Bill that while he lived on a grand scale, when you talked to him in detail about the finances of writing, he had minute knowledge of the most trivial amounts of money coming in and going out, as if he were a struggling writer who had to attend carefully to such things. He knew what magazine paid how much for a piece, for example. His precision about small amounts of money was one reason I was chagrined about the winch handle. I knew he knew down to the penny how much the thing cost. Not that he minded, or would have said he minded, but he knew to the penny.

A long time ago, in 1983, he published a book called *Overdrive*, a journal of a few days in his life. It was a charming and funny piece of work. People loved Bill, or disliked him, and sometimes hated him. In private, he was different from the tongue-flicking public persona he had concocted, the one who drawled and tapped his pencil on his front teeth. People who couldn't stand Bill couldn't bear his book, either.

One of them was Nora Ephron, who reviewed *Overdrive* for the *New York Times*. She accused Bill of being a terrible snob and, in so many words, a dumb, nouveau riche Irishman who, a couple of generations ago, might have kept a pig in his kitchen.

It was not Bill's playing Bach on the harpsichord that offended Nora, or the servants, or the phone calls from the White House when his friend Ronald Reagan lived there. His worst affront in Nora's eyes seemed to be the custom-chopped and -stretched, chauffeur-driven Cadillac with the partition and the special back seat temperature control. It was not even that William F. Buckley Jr. rode around in such a car, like a Mafia don in his land yacht, but rather the way that he wrote about it with a blithe air of *doesn't everyone?* entitlement.

Nora thought one should have the grace to conceal such indulgences, or at least to sound guilty about them. But Bill luxuriated in his amenities, and one heard in his prose the happy sigh of a man sinking into a hot bath.

I think Nora misunderstood both Bill and the nature of his snobbery. Bill Buckley had many enemies, for he was, to use one of Donald Trump's favorite terms of approbation, "a warrior." He was also an expansive character who was entirely democratic in his range of friends and interests. He was the reverse of a snob. He had plenty of friends who disagreed with him politically. He routinely (and secretly) helped people of all conditions, with gifts of money and other kindnesses. When the liberal economist John Kenneth Galbraith, an old friend with whom he disagreed about everything on the political side of things, was in his long decline and unable to leave his house in Cambridge, Massachusetts, Bill regularly took the train up to Boston to visit and talk and ease his loneliness.

The authentic snob is usually a porch with no mansion. Snobbery emerges from an anxiety that the jungles of vulgarity are too close. It is a grasping after little dignities, little validations and reassurances. The writer Sébastien Chamfort located what was surely the ultimate snob, a nameless French gentleman: "A fanatical social climber, observing that all round the Palace of Versailles it stank of urine, told his tenants and servants to come and make water round his château."

22

When I was twelve and thirteen, I worked as a page boy in the US Senate during the summertime. I ran errands among the American gods. We each have our own myth system. I had a child's reverence for the country.

Senator Lyndon Johnson of Texas was minority leader at the time, a gleaming man in monogrammed shirts, and gold cuff links, and Countess Mara neckties, and polished cowboy boots. John Kennedy was the freshman senator from Massachusetts, still on crutches from the back operation that was one of his preliminary brushes with death. He looked like a sloppy, skinny kid at the rear of the Senate chamber, and yet every eye in the place was focused on him, for he had some sort of magic.

The darker Irishman, Senator Joseph McCarthy of Wisconsin, lumbered glowering through democracy's temple in a shiny blue suit. He smelled of alcohol when I rode with him on the monorail subway that ran between the Capitol and the Senate Office Building. Hubert Humphrey was there, too, an overgarrulous old-time leftist idealist who would come to complex grief some years hence, in the sixties, at the hands of the man, Lyndon Johnson, who was then his minority leader. All of the future was hidden from us—assassinations, Vietnam, everything.

They were sleek Olympians then and I spent my days in a sort of heaven: an American Empyrean. The cast of characters was wonderful, and I was Kipling's Kim, indeed. The archaic Southerners (Walter George of Georgia, James Eastland of Mississippi, Rhett Maybank of South Carolina, Earl Long of Louisiana, Harry Byrd of Virginia, Clyde Roark Hoey of North Carolina, who wore wing collars) added up to a tent show of Confederate Shakespeareans: All types were represented, from the aristocratic planter to the old seg Faulknerian cracker. The planters wore Palm Beach suits and carried their proud heads like Romans.

The Senate in those days seemed to bring together all the moods and possibilities, all the physiognomies and styles of dress, all the regional accents, and all the political variations of which the great nation was capable.

Except for the African American variation. There were no black people at all.

My boss was Bobby Baker, Lyndon Johnson's slick young dogsbody from North Carolina, a country boy who made good under Lyndon's patronage. He wore dove-gray pleated silk neckties (a thing I had never seen before and have not seen since) and knew everything about every-body—which senators were drunk and which were sober at voting time, and where each might be found, and who was in bed with whom. He knew which senators were taking big extracurricular money, and how much, and how they were getting it—illegal oil money, for example, would flow in to buy votes for this or that legislation.

One day, former president Herbert Hoover appeared at the back of the Senate chamber. He was by that time an apple-cheeked, smiling old man, a sort of Jack Frost, white haired, his white eyebrows bristling, a ghost of history at last grown old—and unexpectedly merry now that flush times had returned. The Republicans had come back to power with Ike, after two decades of Democrats in the White House, and the disgraced Hoover, who had left town in early 1933 when banks were closing all over the country and the economy had collapsed and people out of work lived in "Hoovervilles," now judged it safe to return. The Republican senators cheered and applauded when they saw the relic who had come among them, not quite in vindication, but almost: He was, shall we say, sheepishly beatified. The senators lined up to shake his hand, and after them, the page boys, including me. I write these lines with a hand that once shook that of Herbert Hoover.

❧

Most mornings, Vice President Richard Nixon sat in the presiding officer's chair, just over my left shoulder as I, dressed in navy blue slacks, a white shirt, and a black knit tie, perched on the steps of the rostrum and waited for the snap of a senator's fingers.

Nixon, just getting up to speed, was an earnest young man with the manner of an older one, a son impersonating a father. His voice was a mellow business executive's basso profundo that, when telling a lie in future years, would become a growl of disavowal. He would waggle his jowls for emphasis, as if, on some dark street of his mind, his own idealized innocence had been outraged. By a sly trick of dissociation, Nixon would emerge, as from a cave or from under a bridge, to defend his own quailing, maiden blamelessness.

Like Eisenhower, Nixon was new at his job. Ike had nearly dropped Nixon from the ticket during his campaign the previous September because, out of the blue, the *New York Post* revealed that as a senator from California, Nixon had been the beneficiary of a slush fund worth some $16,000 or more, organized by some of his well-heeled California backers. The actual purpose of the fund, Nixon insisted, was simply to help him pay for stationery and stamps and certain political expenses, including the high cost of commuting by plane from California to Washington, DC, to keep in touch with his constituents.

I never thought the scandal amounted to much, but there was a great cry among liberals, and Eisenhower, who was sometimes wobbly and opportunistic in his political practice, and who did not like Nixon much anyway (having accepted him as his running mate only to balance the ticket in terms of age and ideology—Ike being a moderate Republican and Nixon an anti-Communist conservative), was on the point of dumping Nixon over the fund.

But Nixon saved himself and added the name of a dog to the political folklore. He went on nationwide television and delivered the Checkers speech, an American classic that in its subtexts and emotional nuances conjured up the world he came from: the Depression, the humiliation of the proud, moneyless American classes, the touch of Norman Rockwell; and the war, the turnaround in the American economy, the postwar boom. Only America had been left prospering out of all the industrial countries, Europe and nearly everywhere else being in ashes—so that

God's verdict on that world struggle was clear enough. If it needed elaboration, Luce's *TIME* and *Life* would explain.

Nixon's pride and touchiness and his talent for sly, cornball self-dramatization were all there on that Tuesday night, drenched in a distinctive black-and-white, 1930s Frank Capra sentimentality. With bleak, defensive-defiant gallantry, he referred to how great his wife, Pat, looked in a "good Republican cloth coat"—which was not, he meant to assure the hardworking people of Bakersfield and East Lansing, a goddamned fancy mink coat of the kind that rich people wore. He wound up waggling his jowls once more and insisting that, "I don't care what anyone says"—his daughters Trisha and Julie would keep the little dog Checkers that an admirer from Texas had given to the family.

There was aggressive and sullen resentment in this, with the admixture of pluckiness and even a muted black Irish rage that smoldered like peat and gleamed in his chinquapin eyes. (House Speaker Sam Rayburn referred to Nixon as "the man with the chinquapin eyes," a nice hayseed reference to chinquapin nuts, which were kin to chestnuts.) The trick was to be a victim, but a defiant one. In the Great Depression, America had been laid low. The world's great power rode the boxcars and struggled to make ends meet; now, Nixon borrowed the moral shine of that 1930s struggle to exonerate himself on a charge of 1950s boodling.

The business about the dog was purest Nixon. No one had suggested that the spaniel should be returned to the people who sent it. Nixon conjured an imaginary danger (a menace to his little girls' happiness, something like the threat by the wicked Kansas neighbor to have Dorothy's dog, Toto, destroyed) and then gallantly interposed his dudgeon: He set himself up as the hero of a cunningly improvised domestic pageant. The Checkers speech, which owed something to the *Perils of Pauline* (with Nixon, Checkers, the girls, and even Pat all playing the part of Pauline), became, so to speak, a pilot sitcom for the decade of the 1950s.

I watched the performance on our black-and-white TV set in the kitchen of the house on Newark Street in Washington, with my mother behind me at the kitchen table muttering, "That phony, that bastard!" Even at the tender age of eleven, I understood the performance in its

tone and implications, in its distinctively middle class–American moral
rhetoric. I return to it now, a lifetime later, as a classic delineation of
certain story lines of American money.

I recognized the still bitter wind of the Depression gusting through
the speech. Pat's "Republican cloth coat" referred back to that privation.
The cold had penetrated whatever thin coats people owned in the thirties; the chill had gotten into their bones, into their marrow, and it might
never leave. The postwar American economy had commenced to boom
and people had cars, suburban homes, air conditioners, barbecues; but
the remnant of the cold fear of the 1930s lingered in the heart. Meantime,
the Cold War (China with its billions of people had gone communist; the
Soviets had the bomb now; Joe McCarthy was loose; and, before long,
the Rosenbergs would be executed) stirred fresher fears and the nuclear
implication.

I was never quite able to dislike Nixon—still less to hate him as my
mother did, smoke coming out of her ears at the mention of his name,
her voice lowering into a Nixonian growl: "That son of a bitch! That son
of a bitch!" She and my father knew him personally, socially, when he
first came to Washington as a congressman in 1947. She got drunk with
him one night at a political dinner and told him to get out of politics.
He didn't like her much after that. He called my father the next morning
and said: "Hugh, can't you control your wife?"

I could not hate Nixon because I picked up in him a bleak resonance
that I recognized: one that had passed through so much of America in
the 1930s.

Nixon's parents, Frank and Hannah—she a devout Quaker—had
struggled in Whittier, running a small grocery and gas station. The emotion with which I sympathized was humiliation: a sullen, chronic ache
in the morale, in the sense of self.

The lack of money produces, especially in a child, an unbearable
sense of unworthiness...and out of the injustice of that humiliation,
a feeling of resentment that may become a permanent aspect of his
character. A country, as well as an individual, may experience such emotions. When Nixon went to Whittier College, he started a club called
the Orthogonians (the squares) in opposition to (and in defiance of)

a club called the Franklins, which was Whittier's fraternity of students from fancier families—the sons of doctors, lawyers, and judges, say, and not of shopkeepers like the Nixons, or plumbers and the like. It's the comparative lack of money and respect that stings—the implication of unworthiness, of inferiority. The basics of democratic doctrine are violated by money. A galling injustice is done, and money can get away with it.

I believe that Watergate, which ended Nixon's presidency, came out of the Great Depression. Watergate originated in a story of personal humiliation because of money, the story of the feelings of cutting shame and resentment and terrible longing that were engendered in Dick Nixon's mind when he was a boy. His mind was formed at least in part by that distinctive 1930s Southern California bleakness. He felt himself looked down upon sometimes, maybe all his life, by the Franklins who came from money; from families like the Kennedys whose boys had trust funds and went to Harvard. and not, God forbid, to Whittier College: rich, good-looking boys who got away with everything.

᳇

Joe DiMaggio was on the cover of the September 20, 1948, issue of *TIME*. The magazine was dense with ads that proclaimed something of the country's postwar idea of itself and the state of its prosperity.

An ad for Burlington Mills had an illustration of an obviously prosperous horseman clearing a jump at an equestrian event: "A touch of the heel, a tightening of the rein, a press of the knee—and the good horse responds, almost as if it had been spoken to. In the world of Fibers, rayon too responds with instant understanding. Specify your lustre, for instance—and rayon responds with dull, semi-dull, or bright."

"Hair getting thin?" asked Ephraim Products.

In a full-page ad for a Lincoln—"Fine-Car Driving"—you saw a bright tomato-red convertible with white sidewall tires, a prosperous young married couple in the front seat. The car is unaccountably parked a couple of feet from a private swimming pool that a woman is getting out of so that she can admire the car.

The meaning of these postwar messages is that the Orthogonians were being invited to entertain the fantasies of Franklins. The immense consumer economy was afoot. Eventually, Dick Nixon of Whittier would have a valet and would develop a taste for expensive French wines. But, at that time, he still walked on the beach in business shoes, something that a Kennedy would not have done, and when Watergate came years later, Nixon would, even in the summertime, seek to comfort himself with the Franklin touch of a fire in the fireplace. He would have them turn on the air conditioner so that he could enjoy the blaze. In Nixon, there was always that odd disjunction, something out of sync in his impulses.

Sometimes when I was a page boy, I would bring a dish of vanilla ice cream to Lyndon Johnson on the Senate floor. I fetched it from the Senate cafeteria downstairs. One day, I had to carry Senator Margaret Chase Smith's handbag across the Capitol to bring it to her on the Senate floor. I ran through the corridors with the bag tucked under my arm like a football—a broken field run among the tourists.

For such work, I was paid $60 a week—an inconceivably handsome sum for a boy of my age at that time. I had found El Dorado. It was the United States Capitol.

We collected our pay, in cash, every two weeks at a window in the Senate Disbursing Office in the basement of the Capitol.

To my amazement, I was told that that if I wished, I could be paid every two weeks with 120 silver dollars. I never tried it. I thought that if I did, the coins would be so heavy in my pockets that my trousers would fall off.

Years later, when I thought of the silver dollars, I remembered that Lycurgus the lawgiver of ancient Sparta wanted his people's money to be as unwieldy as, say, cattle—and as difficult to negotiate. He ordained that Sparta's money should take the form of large, heavy iron coins.

According to Plutarch, Lycurgus wished to encourage equality among the Spartans, and to suppress luxury, and greed, and dependence on money. He wanted to isolate Sparta from outside trade, from foreign influence and the decadence that it might bring. He forbade the use of gold and silver. He introduced *pelanor*s, pieces of iron that were intrinsically worthless, bulky, and hard to transport.

(Many centuries later, in the Transatlantic slave trade, most transactions were recorded in units called "barrs"—literally the monetary equivalent of iron bars. A yard of cloth was worth one bar, a barrel of rum ten bars. A slave's worth would be calculated accordingly.)

Sparta's warrior society actually encouraged stealing; it was one of the manly arts that a boy ought to learn. The 19th-century French anarchist Pierre-Joseph Proudhon would demonize the thought with his famous "La propriété, c'est le vol!" (Property is theft!) The Spartan people's money, identity, and character were densely intertwined. So it has been with Americans and their money.

Was Lycurgus right to want to make money scarce and impossible to wield? Is money a disaster, a catastrophe? Has it become the root of all evil in new ways—evil, for example, as an environmental disaster? Is money as consumerism the great villain of the world now?

Or, on the contrary, is money the salvation of which the pandemic and such would deprive us?

Is money a miracle or a disaster?

❧

History decided against Lycurgus. In the 21st century, money is global and as fast and light as electrons. Paper bills are almost an atavism; coins belong to an earlier age. To pay with cash seems primitive.

Amazon has announced plans to deliver packages by drone—so that consumer goods will fly through the air almost as fast as money—and before long, having been "consumed," the ruins of the goods will find their way, by truck or scow, to landfills or to ocean deeps and shallows, where they will coalesce into new mountain ranges and oceanic garbage patches and wait (for centuries, eons perhaps) to decompose.

The 21st century is an un-Spartan and anti-Lycurgan universe altogether—of plastic cards, and Bluetooth blips, and flashing, entirely notional and invisible transactions: Money has become a dust of electrons, upon whose moods and phantom motions civilizations rise and fall and rise.

The unbearable lightness of money.

&

Money is a way of thinking, as language is a way of thinking. Money translates the world and its commodities and products—and nearly everything else—into codes of value and allows the world to communicate in terms immediately intelligible. This Ford Fusion sells for $27,655 and that Mercedes sedan goes for $57,899, and we know precisely where we stand in relation to both cars—values (price tags) that we coordinate in relation to our own means: income, budget, and so on. To that extent, money is an admirably orderly asset to civilization.

Years ago, I knew an endearing man who was a writer at *TIME* magazine. He was given to drinking quantities of Gordon's gin. Now and then when he got drunk, he would talk late at night about how, as a Marine rifleman in his youth, he had gone ashore at Guadalcanal and fought in the jungles. He did not talk about the Japanese or about the horrors of combat, but rather about how he became obsessed by the spectacle in those jungles of simultaneous generation and decay: It was all mixed together, he said—the tremendous and spontaneous proliferation of life in millions of teeming forms and, simultaneously, the orgy of death and decay. Life and death were all mixed up with each other, so that they became indistinguishable. The lives and deaths of Japanese soldiers and US Marines dramatized the principle, for they were all young men with everything to live for, raging through the jungles of a Pacific island and killing and mutilating one another.

"It made no sense to me," he would say. It was not that the killing made no sense; it was rather that the two principles converging on Guadalcanal (nature rotting and breeding simultaneously, as if it could not make up its mind as to which was its proper business) seemed to him a cosmic contradiction. Or that's what he said. There would then be a melodramatic pause and sip of Gordon's gin. "It was then that I discovered the madness of God."

The simultaneity of generation and decay is also manifest in the global consumer economy: An overwhelming inventory of products turns into an overwhelming inventory of waste. Money is a biological phenomenon, and its life-forms flourish and decay in the complex economy of the world.

23

In his time (the middle years of the 20th century), people called Henry Luce the most influential private citizen in America. It was said that Luce, as the publisher of *TIME*, *Life*, and other magazines, had more impact on the American mind than the country's entire system of public education.

Luce envisioned a journalism of the ongoing Creation: It necessarily included an account of the doings of power; the works of Caesar and of politics; the *res publica* as it unfolded, moment to moment, in the onrushing drama of the world. Luce liked Big Ideas.

James Agee, who also harbored Big Ideas, groped toward a journalism that would amount to nothing less than a philosophy of cognition.

In 1936, *Fortune* sent Agee, along with the photographer Walker Evans, to investigate the lives of Alabama sharecroppers. Ultimately, *Fortune* did not publish the result of that four-week expedition. Agee would turn it into a four-hundred-page speculation on the Condition of Man, written in an elaborate prose that was faux-Elizabethan and faux-Faulknerian—a hybrid work that combined brilliant observation with turgid, unreadable speculations and strange spasms of Agee's Anglican conscience. It was finally published four years later as a book, *Let Us Now Praise Famous Men*. By then, Agee had left *Fortune*. Later, he would return to the Luce fold as a writer and film critic at *TIME*.

Let Us Now Praise Famous Men amounted to metaphysical or mystical journalism—sometimes wonderful. If Luce, the son of Presbyterian missionaries, a connoisseur of Sunday sermons, emphasized the ongoing Creation, Agee was concerned with something else—the holiness and innocence of individual lives; the practice of journalism as a pure,

Christian, Mount of Olives act of imaginative and suffering sympathy with the poor; their griefs, their confusions, the poignancy of their meager and threadbare lives. Agee descended from New York to Alabama as if in imitation of Christ, who came down from heaven to Galilee. Agee lived among the sharecroppers as Christ lived among men, although, in fairness, Agee made no messianic claims for himself.

As close observation—granular journalism—Agee's performance was sometimes breathtaking. There were moments, years later, when Norman Mailer worked in the same vein, involving himself in the story and swooping around the cosmos in extravagant metaphors, stunt flying. Tom Wolfe worked some of the same effects, in his own extravagant style. *Let Us Now Praise Famous Men* was a precursor to the New Journalism of the 1960s.

Agee explained his idea of his journalistic assignment:

> Here at the center is a creature: it would be our business to show
> how through every instant of every day of every year of his existence
> alive he is from all sides streamed inward upon, bombarded, pierced,
> destroyed by that enormous sleeting of all objects forms and ghosts
> how great how small no matter, which surround and whom his
> senses take in, in as great and perfect and exact particularity as we
> can name them.

His subject was the white Alabama sharecropper—a victim, a man acted upon, beaten down, impoverished in the midst of the Great Depression that was the work of dark malign forces, the Overlords.

Agee's deeper theme had something to do with American innocence. He found in the sharecroppers a suffering Christian American innocence purified by its poignant, bleak, sweetly human passivity and bewilderment.

The implied American innocence and authenticity of Luce's Oskaloosa, Iowa—his wished-for hometown—was quite a different thing from Agee's Alabama. Oskaloosa was not impoverished but rather, blamelessly self-sufficient and middle class. Oskaloosa would have a Chamber of Commerce, an Elks Lodge, and a 4-H Club, and the people there, on the whole, would pay their bills and eat well, though simply, and would know how to keep their homes warm when the Blue Northers swept down from the high plains in January, and how to take shelter when tornadoes made woozy cones on the horizon. The innocence of Agee's Alabama sharecropper, on the other hand, would be that of purest vulnerable humanity—a suffering peasant holiness.

Luce's American innocence was small-town bourgeois and had some of the Norman Rockwell sentimentality. Luce responded to Elbert Hubbard's idea of a pristine American ignition—of hayseed geniuses, like, say, Henry Ford, raised on a Michigan farm, a shrewd natural tinkerer who, like the Wright Brothers, would transform the world. In actuality, Henry Ford hated the farm when he was growing up and could not wait to get away from it, but later would idealize the rural America that he had done so much to transform, and nostalgically collected McGuffey Readers and put them in a museum. The McGuffeys themselves belonged to a notion of the old innocence, like the little red schoolhouse or Laura Wilder's *Little House on the Prairie*.

In words that might have disconcerted his editors in New York, Agee wrote of his Alabama assignment:

This would be our business, to show them each [the sharecroppers and their families] thus transfixed as between the stars' trillions of javelins and of each the transfixions: but it is beyond my human power to do. The most I can do—the most I can hope to do—is to make a number of physical entities as plain and vivid as possible, and to make a few guesses, a few conjectures; and to leave to you much of the burden of realizing in each of them what I have wanted to make clear of them as a whole, how each is itself, and how each is a sharpener.

We undertake not much yet some, to say: to say, what is his house; for whom does he work; under what arrangements and in what results: what is this work; who is he and where from, that he is now here, what is it his life has been and has done to him; what of his wife and of their children, each; for all of these each is a life, a full universe: what are their clothes; what food is theirs to eat; what is it

which is in their senses and their minds: what is the living and manner of their day, of a season, of a year: what inward and outward, is
their manner of living, of their spending and usage of these few years'
openness out of the black vast and senseless death; what is their manner of life. (sic, throughout)

Agee's agenda, though grandiloquent, was what any intelligent journalist hopes to achieve when going out on an assignment of the kind
that the editors of *Fortune* gave him. It was an imaginative and generous
and thoughtful idea for a story—and unusual for a business magazine
whose principle audience was corporate executives; ultimately the assignment produced a big, strange book that is here and there unreadable but
nonetheless has moments of greatness. Walker Evans's accompanying
black-and-white photographs are magnificent.

Whatever greatness the book may have is the result not of Agee's
balance as a journalist in any traditional sense but of his alert, observant
eye in partnership with an overabundance of heart and his extravagant
metaphysical literary inclination: A reader may admire the art of the book,
and the inner truths it gropes for, and yet be aware of its tremendous
objective omissions.

Agee disdained journalism. And he disdained Henry Luce. Once, in
the early 1930s, in the first days of *Fortune* magazine, young Agee sat in
his office in the Chrysler Building late at night listening to Beethoven
on a record player, as he often did, and suffering over a story, perhaps
with the help of the bottle of bourbon that he kept in the desk drawer.
He distracted himself with a fantasy. He imagined that he had a pistol,
and that he would walk out of his office and down the corridor to Luce's
office. He would enter. He would confront Luce, sitting at his desk, and
shoot him in the chest. Hearing the shot, all the writers and researchers
up and down the corridor would peek out of their offices and, when they
realized what had happened, clap their hands and cheer like munchkins
when they saw that the wicked witch was dead. (This was, however, some
years before the movie of *The Wizard of Oz* was made).

Agee considered himself a poet and he regarded journalism—especially journalism for Henry Luce's magazine, paid for by Luce's capitalist

money—to be a form of moral slumming and even a cause for shame. He wished to redeem the shame either by denying he was doing the work at all or by transforming it into Higher Art. In the latter, he in part succeeded.

He wrote:

> I do not wish to appear to speak favorably of journalism. I have never yet seen a piece of journalism which conveyed more than the slightest fraction of what any even moderately reflective and sensitive person would mean and intend by those unachievable words, and that fraction itself I have never seen clean of one or another degree of patent, to say nothing of essential, falsehood. Journalism is true in the sense that everything is true to the state of being and is what con-ditioned and produced it (which is also, but less so perhaps, a limita-tion of art and science): but that is about as far as its value goes. This is not to accuse or despise journalism for anything beyond its own complacent delusion, and its enormous power to poison the public with the same delusion, that it is telling the truth even of what it tells of. Journalism can within its own limits be "good" or "bad," "true" or "false," but it is not in the nature of journalism even to approach any less relative degree of truth....
>
> The very blood and semen of journalism, on the contrary, is a broad and successful form of lying. Remove that form of lying and you no longer have journalism.

It is interesting to read Agee's rant on journalism in the midst of the Fake News era of the 21st century, and at the same time to recall that Agee wrote his words at a moment when Hitler's Nazis had put books into bonfires and Goebbels's labors were far advanced in the propagation of the titanic lies and myths—of the *Volk* and *Kultur*, of the bestiality and inhumanity of Jews, and of Aryan superiority—that plunged the planet into a world war that killed fifty million people. The self-proclaimed Communist Agee composed his meditations on journalism at a time when Stalin was conducting his show trials in Moscow. The trials came only a few years after Stalin had starved some ten million Ukrainian kulaks in the Great Famine. Agee wrote during the time that George Orwell was in Barcelona fighting on the Loyalist side in the Spanish Civil War and discovering that his idealistic pro-Communist sympathies were misplaced. After Orwell caught a Red agent from Moscow in an outrageous lie, he calmly remarked later on: "It was the first time I encountered this kind of professional lying—except of course for the professional lying by journalists." In certain classes and modes of knowingness, then as now, it was assumed that all journalists lie all the time.

At the moment that Agee's book was published, Henry Luce was working hard to persuade Americans to end their isolation and join the fight against Hitler. Just as Agee's book came out, all of Western Europe except the British Isles was overrun by the Nazis. Britain barely held out. In England, Edward R. Murrow and his team of correspondents did first-class work in bringing home to Americans the dangers and the realities. Vincent Sheehan and Dorothy Thompson, both distinguished American journalists, had been reporting all through the thirties about the Hitler danger.

In Soviet Russia in the early thirties, a young correspondent for what was then known as the *Manchester Guardian*, Malcolm Muggeridge, reported back to the West on the realities and horrors of Stalin's Great Famine—even as the Moscow correspondent for the *New York Times*, Walter Duranty, had won the Pulitzer Prize for his series reporting what a splendid job Stalin was doing. In China, Theodore White, Luce's young correspondent in Chongqing, was reporting on the Honan famine that killed millions and on the realities of the tremendous Chinese struggle between the Kuomintang and the Communists. At the same time, the Japanese were committing almost unprecedented atrocities, notably the "rape of Nanking."

Agee's groping and grandiose religious mind considered variations on these themes: What is the American innocence? What is the American guilt?

If the innocent and vulnerable were white Alabama sharecroppers, then where did that leave the matter of Southern white racism? Agee's sharecroppers were saints and martyrs, in his meditation on them. But, objectively speaking, some were also redneck racists. This was inconvenient.

H. L. Mencken—jaunty, cackling, irresponsible, brilliant—wrote of the Southern whites as morons, imbeciles, brain-damaged bigots, slack-jawed primitives.

Agee was extravagant in the opposite direction. His sharecroppers' innocence was conditioned upon their abject powerlessness. They had no power. They had no money. They were at the mercy of the elements and of the landlords who did have money and power.

Yet the sharecroppers were white, and as powerless as they were, they had more power than the blacks, who dwelt, for present purposes, on the margins of Agee's story. In journalism, the story line is everything. Agee somewhat averted his gaze, or else plunged back into his *own* sense of guilt, which was, after all, the environment in which his spirit and prose style seemed to flourish. He did not mind styling himself as somewhat crucified, and that poignancy drew attention away from the complex objective facts of blacks and whites in the stricken agricultural South of the Great Depression.

And yet, Agee offered a moment, a magnificent scene, that did justice to the black side of that story. It was only a glimpse, but an indelible one.

Agee, first arriving with Walker Evans, was on a lonely rural road. A happy and attractive young black couple walked down the road, shy and very much in love. They saw the white man and grew nervous and went past him, but Agee—wishing to ask them a perfectly innocent question, something about directions—followed them, walking fast. They became aware of him and, as he continued to walk rapidly toward them, they were seized by a tremendous terror, as if the oldest horror haunting the rural South was about to be reenacted...

Agee caught the moment perfectly.

24

The philanthropic model that was judged to be outmoded in the emergency years of the New Deal returns, with a certain pertinence, and even a moral purity, in the globalized context of the 21st century. In the absence of a worldwide system of relief of the kind that Franklin Roosevelt invented for America, the global, supra-governmental designs of philanthropist billionaires like Bill Gates make sense. They operate, at their best, with a flexibility and global range that is impossible, or far more difficult, for government aid programs or United Nations agencies.

The Gates model—pooling billionaires' enormous contributions to do targeted good on a planetary scale—might globalize Cotton Mather's American principle, the idea of two oars rowing to heaven. Gates's notion is the enlistment of big money—the biggest—in a global performance of entrepreneurial good. If that model worked, the conflict between God and Mammon would wither away.

After every devastation—after the San Francisco earthquake of 1906, say, or after the flattening of Japan and Germany in 1945—there comes (if all goes well) a great rebuilding. The calamity leaves a clean slate, upon which reinventing minds may exercise their entrepreneurial imaginations and visionary wits.

After the pandemic, how will America reinvent itself?

EPILOGUE

The last sentence of *The Great Gatsby* became well known—one of those Fitzgerald fragments, half-poetry, with a smudge of the mystical upon them: "So we beat on, boats against the current, borne back ceaselessly into the past."

Odd, I thought. Americans, by temperament and everything else, are more apt to be borne ceaselessly into the future, aren't they?

The truth is that the American tide is variable; it runs in and it runs out again, carrying the country's mind in either direction, depending on moods and the pull of the moon.

The nostalgia, the longing, may sometimes be religious and chivalric, and it was present even when the country was much younger, when Henry David Thoreau wrote that mysterious line in *Walden*: "I long ago lost a hound, a bay horse and a turtle dove, and I am still on their trail."

What did it mean?

"Make America Great Again" is a thought that also refers to the past. But the nostalgia here is Thermidorian—hard, truculent. The greatness that was, by God, shall be again.

These are different notes played on different American instruments to produce different emotional or political or historical effects. Napoleon said history is merely a fable agreed upon; in the 21st century, Americans cannot agree on their own fable, and that is the entire source of their trouble.

I remember something that the photographer (and Agee's collaborator) Walker Evans said about the past. One day in New Haven, the art critic Hilton Kramer, a friend of his, urged Evans to write a memoir. Evans replied that he would never do so: If he wrote such a book, it would be "all lies." He said, "You can't write anything but lies about the past."

That is not entirely true. In any case, our time may prove that it is impossible to write anything but lies about the present.

Ashley Wilkes, played by Leslie Howard in *Gone with the Wind*, was a supreme elegist of the dreamland, the Walter Scott Confederacy (that immense fable agreed upon)—especially in the second half of the story, after the burning of Atlanta and the end of the Civil War. By that point, the past was in ruins, and the job was to start over, to make money in new ways—to rebuild. Scarlett O'Hara adapted herself to the task. She became a ruthless capitalist. She employed convict labor in her Atlanta lumber mill in the same spirit of business, red in tooth and claw, that animated John Brown of Providence when he sent ships to the Windward Coast in quest of slaves.

&

I sit at my farm now, tapping away at the last of this. I have not seen the red fox since that morning when COVID set in.

I glanced at the screens a moment ago and saw that the Dow had fallen another 500 points, heading south on another little wave of fear. Tomorrow the wave will recede. Epidemiologists warn that this may go on and on.

Gone with the Wind has just been banned from streaming on HBO because of the movie's racial stereotypes. Confederate statues are coming down everywhere, and Confederate flags are banned—by the US Marines, by NASCAR.

&

Two famous exit lines—one from *The Great Gatsby* and one from *Gone with the Wind*—float into my mind. The first, Fitzgerald's, speaks of the past: "So we beat on, boats against the current, born back ceaselessly into the past."

The second opens onto the future.

Scarlett O'Hara says, "Tomorrow is another day."

That much, at least, is true.

We have had enough of the past.
We have had far too much of the present.
Into what strange world will the future lead us?
And will it be wonderful?

ACKNOWLEDGMENTS

I wrote *God and Mammon* as part of my work as the Henry Grunwald senior fellow at the Ethics and Public Policy Center in Washington, DC. The fellowship is named for the extraordinary man who was the managing editor of *TIME* and, after that, the editor in chief of TIME Inc., occupying Henry Luce's old chair. Henry Grunwald is my favorite among the many editors I have worked with in a long career. I am deeply grateful to Louise Grunwald for establishing the fellowship and supporting it so generously. I owe a debt of gratitude to Tom and Alice Tisch, who have been immensely helpful in funding the work. I owe thanks as well to my old friend from *TIME*, Jonathan Z. Larsen.

Some passages in this book were adapted from essays of mine that appeared in the *Wall Street Journal*, *City Journal*, and *National Review*. My thanks especially to James Taranto at *WSJ*.

I am most grateful to Ed Whelan and my colleagues at the Ethics and Public Policy Center for their friendship and for what I can only call the distinguished sanity of their work in a time that is anything but sane.